WORSHIP PLANNING
RESOURCES FOR
EVERY SUNDAY OF THE YEAR

THE

ABINGDON WORSHIP

ANNUAL 2022

EDITED BY
MARY SCIFRES
AND B. J. BEU

ABINGDON PRESS / NASHVILLE

The Abingdon Worship Annual 2022

Copyright© 2021 by Abingdon Press

ISBN 978-1-7910-1066-9

21 22 23 24 25 26 27 28 29 30—10 9 8 7 6 5 4 3 2 1

MANUFACTURED IN THE UNITED STATES OF AMERICA

Contents

April

May

June

July

August

September

October

November

December

Introduction

Planning Virtual Worship Pandemic or Not!

Until the global pandemic of 2020, very few of our readers had been planning worship for the virtual world. Some of us livestreamed or recorded worship services for our homebound members, but very few of us put much thought into those virtual options in our creative thinking and planning. Now, almost all of us do. With that in mind, B. J. and I offer some insights and ideas to you, gleaned from your colleagues around the world.

Versions of Virtual Worship

There are many ways of worshipping together, even while worshipping in our homes. For years, homebound and traveling church members have yearned to stay connected with their church families. Now, almost all of us have developed methods for staying connected through our computers, tablets, and phones. We hope you will continue connecting in these virtual ways, even when the dangers of a pandemic have passed. The more we can connect without regard to geography, the more inclusive our worship services and congregational relationships can be. Imagine how much joy we bring our homebound "visitors" when they stream worship right into their living rooms and assisted living apartments. To stay "connected" in the past, my homebound grandmother had to rely on copies of *The Upper Room* and visits from her pastor. Now, all who can't attend Sunday worship can stay connected with your congregation, thanks to modern technology and the church's amazing willingness and ability to adapt in 2022!

As the pandemic spread around our globe, we watched colleagues without the ability to livestream create amazing possibilities from their smartphones, camcorders, and tablets. The following methods categorize some of the ways you have made virtual worship possible for your people.

1. Prerecorded worship filmed in "one take"—weekly sermons, musical offerings, and so on
2. Prerecorded worship filmed separately in various segments from multiple leaders and locations—distributed as individual elements
3. Prerecorded worship filmed separately in various segments from multiple leaders and locations—edited and distributed as a complete recorded worship service
4. Prerecorded musical offerings filmed from multiple participants and locations—edited into a virtual choir or ensemble
5. Livestreamed sermons, meditations, or devotions
6. Livestreamed worship services, inclusive of sermon, music, and liturgy
7. Video conference worship, using a service like Zoom, to allow for interaction and fellowship in the worship experience

We applaud you for creating such beautiful worship in so many innovative ways! Below, we take a closer look at each of the methods noted above.

Prerecorded worship, weekly sermons, and musical offerings that are filmed in "one take" can be done with a simple smartphone, computer, or basic recording camera. For best results recording with a phone or video, purchase a simple tripod or stand to provide stability for the camera and allow the leader to focus on the words or music you are offering. The one take option, while not as polished as edited versions, allows for both simplicity and authenticity. Be honest with your congregation that this recording is essentially "live," even though it's prerecorded. Be honest with yourself that the one take option leaves you more vulnerable as a leader than edited versions. This option frees up an enormous amount of time and cost over methods requiring extensive editing so that worship isn't the only ministry you have the time or money to provide in a given week. For distribution and communication ideas, see the next paragraph.

Prerecorded worship filmed in various segments from multiple leaders and locations that are distributed as individual elements allows diverse and varied worship moments to be shared with your fellowship throughout the week, rather than as a single service. One pastor walked his deserted streets the first week communities were sheltering at home as his videographer recorded him with a drone video camera. The voiceover (added later) was both haunting and comforting as the pastor shared both his concerns and his hopes for his congregation and our world. Another pastor recorded all of her summer sermons from her dock, with a beautiful lake in the background, taking her congregation through a series of "lakeshore" stories of Jesus and the disciples. In both cases, their churches also distributed links to instrumental and vocal music from their church musicians. One church included weekly links to children's messages from volunteers in their Christian education program. When individuals use their own equipment to record these segments, the quality can vary widely. Some churches address this issue by having participants visit the sanctuary at scheduled times so that a videographer can record each segment, or they advise participants in use of common equipment and methods. For example, one church asks each volunteer who records a prayer or song to record it horizontally on a smartphone, using the phone's built-in microphone. Some church administrators and pastors share the links to the various recordings on the church website or in emails with PDF documents. Others post each segment on their social media channels as the segment is created, which allows for spiritual nurture throughout the week. Others wait and send all of the links in a weekly post to create a more unified feel to worship, even when it is created in different segments. Consider sharing prayers and readings from this resource with a variety of volunteer and staff worship leaders throughout your worship year, to expand both participation and creativity in the worship experience. Remind them they are permitted to adapt, edit, or use the resources exactly as they are written in both written and recorded format. Just note the authorship and copyright notice in whatever written communication accompanies your recordings.

Prerecorded worship filmed in various segments from multiple leaders and locations that is edited into one worship service provides a fuller and more familiar worship experience for congregants. As with the previous style, recording from various locations provides a great deal of creativity and variety, but varying sound levels and quality of recordings can present a challenge for your video editor.

Most churches find that the editing is simplified if all recordings are shot in one location using the same equipment, with leaders scheduled at various times to provide for safe physical distancing. This option requires more preparation and planning, along with a paid editor or very generous volunteer who can handle the demands of postproduction editing. Our son Michael Beu, a video editor, works with a number of churches and pastors to manage the technical and time-consuming demands of editing and posting their worship videos, or helps them find volunteers or train staff members to do so. This extra help allows pastors to focus on worship rather than on technology, and many church donors have stepped up to provide the financial support necessary for this new way of providing worship and spiritual nurture.

For the worship experience, some churches "premiere" worship services put together in this way by scheduling the uploaded video to go live at a specific time on their social media channel. This allows and encourages congregants to watch and worship "together" at the same time from their various locations, and also can provide viewers the opportunity for interactive chat on the social media channel, creating a sense of community. This sense of community is increased if the worship service is followed by a virtual fellowship time via video conferencing on platforms like Zoom or Skype. Others "open" the posted worship service video immediately, once editing and uploading is complete, so that worshippers can view and worship whenever they want. One of our readers prefers this latter option, so that her church can join for virtual fellowship and sermon conversation during the normal Sunday morning worship time, having viewed worship the day before.

Prerecorded musical offerings filmed from multiple participants and locations that are edited into a virtual choir or ensemble allow vocal music and ensemble music to continue to be a part of our lives. Solo offerings, however, are much more common because they are more easily achieved with simple recording devices—sometimes connected directly to an electronic musical instrument, other times recorded with the internal microphone provided on the recording device. Most musicians prefer the higher quality of recording with an external microphone, attached to the video recording device. Virtual ensembles require a great deal of postproduction sound editing. It's harder than it looks and sounds, so very few churches choose this option, unless they have a professional studio or advanced sound and video technicians available to them.

Livestreamed sermons, meditations, or devotionals are being offered by churches at all times of day and night around our globe. They can be recorded and offered on almost any social media channel by clicking on their live stream option. One colleague records a daily devotional video, but also posts it in written format on his Facebook page. (He also enlists church leaders to record on Fridays and Saturdays, so he can enjoy sabbath and family time on those days.) Consider using prayers and responsive readings from this resource to enhance devotionals, sermons, or reflective meditations you are providing for your people.

Livestreamed worship services that include sermons, music, and liturgy require recording equipment connected to a live streaming service and, ideally, a wired connection to the internet. Most churches who choose this option have invested considerable money into a streaming broadcast system and have budget for trained staff members who know how to operate both the recording and broadcasting systems. As with the virtual choir option, this isn't as easy as it looks! But it is a beautiful option for churches that have the ability and the resources. That said, most churches who were streaming before the pandemic have both adapted and improved their livestream worship ministry. Before the pandemic, much of livestreamed worship was either an afterthought of what was already happening on Sundays, or a polished "performance." Now, some of the fanciest livestreams have become the simplest. There is an elegance to this simplicity and this intentionality, when worship is crafted to focus on one primary theme or message. Worship services have been shortened to adapt to the shorter attention span of a virtual congregation. Messages and musical offerings are less polished and more personal, creating intimacy and relationship with viewers at home. Don't be fooled, though! The technology in the background to make livestreaming successful is complex with little room for error, which occurs frequently for a variety of reasons. Those of us who livestream on a regular basis have learned to laugh at ourselves, forgive technology, and patiently await our technicians to address the glitches that inevitably arise. One colleague laughingly posted on our clergy Facebook group, "It's time to designate a 'Glitch Sunday!'"

Video conference worship, using providers like Zoom, provides opportunities for interaction and fellowship during the worship experience. While this format creates a more collaborative environment, it requires more flexibility and informality for both leaders and participants. Best practice for this format has participants and members log onto the video conference *with a private church link* in order to prevent interruptions by internet trolls. Designate a video conference coordinator to welcome guests, help with password and technology challenges, monitor chat questions or comments, and mute everyone but the participants once worship begins. A video conference coordinator allows pastors, musicians, and worship leaders to focus on their worship responsibilities without having to control the service's complicated technical requirements.

When the pastor and designated leaders are leading, their video feeds should be the only ones with active microphones. This allows people to hear more clearly and participate more fully without interrupting the worship flow. While microphones are muted, congregational singing, unison and responsive readings, and responses to the Spirit are all possible in this format. If you have a solo worship leader, make sure their microphone is always unmuted so that they can lead the singing, readings, and prayers. To add an interactive component, encourage people to comment in their chat box, or even invite conversation following the message by designating a time of unmuted sermon feedback and Q & A. Similarly, community prayer and joys and concerns can be interactive by unmuting members for these worship elements; but be sure to mute the members again before praying the pastoral or Lord's Prayer. Although you can use a webinar format instead, webinars are more "presentation" than "participation," similar to a Facebook Live or YouTube Premiere.

Choosing or Changing Your Version of Virtual Worship

Several decisions need to be made before settling on a method of virtual worship:

1. Whom is God calling your church to reach? What technology are they able and willing to access?
2. What type of worship experience will best serve the congregation you are called to reach?
3. How much is your church able and willing to spend, both in time and money?
4. What technology and distribution platform best address these questions.

With these decisions in mind, you are ready to work with your worship team to create a virtual worship design and choose a platform best suited to your current needs. What you started with need not limit where you go in 2022 and beyond. Similarly, if you've been doing this alone for the last year and a half, you need not continue doing it alone. This is the perfect time to create a worship team that will work with you, supporting and strengthening both the process and creativity of your worship experience. When planned and implemented alone, virtual worship is already leading to many early retirements and departures from ministry. The workload is simply too exhausting and isolating an experience to sustain by one individual, regardless of how talented they are. Reach out to your leadership, your colleagues, and even community partners to find the help you need. If you're reading this article but not on the worship team, check with your pastor or musician to see if they need support and help. Contact us if you need help figuring out how to find and work with a team.

Adapting Music and Liturgy for Social Distancing and Safety

One of the greatest challenges in church worship today has been the limitations placed on vocal music and the spoken word to avoid spreading infection. Yet, limitations give rise to creativity and new ways for musicians to stay involved in ministry. Some vocal choirs have transitioned into bell choirs. Other vocalists have been reading the texts of favorite hymns or anthems, while instrumentalists play the music underneath. Some churches are prerecording vocal music for presentation on screen during live worship, while simultaneously streaming the live worship and the prerecorded music for their virtual worshippers. Responsive and unison readings are not always the safest option for a congregation gathered together, but two readers may "duet" a responsive reading from the chancel while remaining safely distanced from both worshippers and one another. Or again, music might enhance a solo voice reciting the Lord's Prayer. Looking for more creative ideas? Visit **maryscifres.com** to find some of the creative ways B. J. and Mary are working to address the changing forms of worship.

Adapting Virtual Worship to a Hybrid Form

Over these last few years, you have likely led worship in a variety of ways, adapting to social restrictions the pandemic has thrown our way. As churches reopen their sanctuaries, while also offering virtual worship, we have begun calling this new both-and situation *hybrid worship*. Our worship services are no longer just the old fossil-fueled combustion engine of sanctuary worship, but also electric-fueled worship of videos streamed directly into the homes of church members and friends around the globe. One California colleague is helping his newest member from North Carolina get acquainted with her California church family three thousand miles away. When their sanctuary reopens, she will still be worshipping from her North Carolina living room, utilizing the gifts of this hybrid worship model to nourish her spiritual journey across the miles. As congregations again gather for in-person worship, this hybrid model allows us to continue serving our virtual worshippers. To prepare for this, worship leaders have put tech crews in place who can record the services, upload to an online platform, and communicate with the congregation how to access the online service. Your best practice is for worship leaders to focus on the worship components (music, message, liturgy) and for tech and administrative team members to focus on the technology and communication components. Let us know if you have questions or concerns we can help you address, or if you have insights and ideas to share with others.

Mary Scifres and B. J. Beu
admin@maryscifres.com

January 1, 2022

Watch Night/New Year
B. J. Beu

Color

White

Scripture Readings

Ecclesiastes 3:1-13; Psalm 8; Revelation 21:1-6a;
Matthew 25:31-46

Theme Ideas

Start with the end in mind. Where are we going, and
how do we get there? Matthew reminds us that our
actions have eternal consequences. If we truly want to
change our lives, we are charged to feed the hungry,
clothe the naked, visit the sick and imprisoned, and
comfort those who mourn. The new heaven and new
earth may be in our midst, but if we want to be part of
it, we need to treat each other lovingly. In Ecclesiastes,
God reminds us that weeping, tearing down, and lying
fallow will always be part of the seasons and rhythms of
life. As we look with anticipation to the new year ahead,
we place our trust in the one whose glory is beheld in

the new heaven and new earth—the one who will wipe away every tear.

Invitation and Gathering

Centering Words (Ecclesiastes 3)
Through the seasons of life, God walks with us— laughing with us at our follies and foibles, dancing with us in our triumphs, weeping with us in our losses, strengthening us in times of trial. As a new year dawns, know that you never walk alone.

Call to Worship (Ecclesiastes 3, Psalm 8, Matthew 25)
A new day dawns.
> **How majestic is God's name**
> **throughout the earth.**
A new season of life begins.
> **God's glory shines in the heavens**
> **and shimmers on the waters.**
A new year calls us into Christ's glorious future.
> **We will feed the hungry, clothe the naked,**
> **visit the sick and imprisoned,**
> **and see Christ in every face we meet.**

Opening Prayer (Psalm 8, Matthew 25)
Source of love and mercy,
> as we enter a new year in the life of this church,
> > may our love for you be made known
> > > in our love for one another.
Help us leave old grievances in the past
> and former arguments behind,
> > as we open our hearts
> > > to the possibilities that lie before us.

Guide our footsteps into the glory of your ways,
    that we may live as beloved children
        crowned with glory and honor.
May our worship this day
    reflect the greatness of our calling
        and the glory of our heritage. Amen.

Proclamation and Response

Prayer of Yearning (Psalm 8, Matthew 25, Revelation 21)

God of memory and promise,
    your new heaven and new earth
        call us to be more than we have become.
We yearn to enter into fullness of life.
We strive to leave behind our self-centered ways,
    focusing instead on those who suffer from hunger,
        and those who grow weak from lack of shelter
        and warmth.
Curb our temptation to lift up our eyes
    from the homeless and the needy,
        even as we delight in the starry heavens
        and the wonder of your creation.
Set our gaze on the welfare of others,
    that we may live with newfound joy
        in the promise of your new heaven
        and your new earth. Amen.

Words of Assurance (Psalm 8)

The psalmist questions,
    What is the human race that God is mindful of us?
    Who are we that God cares for us so deeply?

In loving delight, you answer,
>   You are my children,
>   whom I have made but a little lower than myself.
> I have crowned you with glory and honor,
>   and I will always love you.

Passing the Peace of Christ (Matthew 25)

Christ comes to us hidden in the sunken eyes of hungry children, the doleful eyes of the sick and imprisoned, and the humiliated eyes of the naked. When we learn to see Christ in these eyes, and then respond accordingly, we find the peace that passes all understanding. Let us gain a taste of this peace, as we see Christ in the hidden hurts of one another. As we share this peace today, we bring the peace of Christ to those in our midst.

Introduction to the Word (Ecclesiastes 3, Matthew 25)

For every thing there is a season.
May this be a season of new possibilities,
>   as we reflect on God's call to feed the hungry,
>   clothe the naked, visit the sick and imprisoned,
>   and comfort those who mourn.

Response to the Word (Ecclesiastes 3)

As we journey through life,
>   **God is always with us.**
In seasons of rejoicing,
>   **we do not laugh alone.**
In seasons of mourning,
>   **we do not weep alone.**
In this season of faithful,
>   **we discover Christ,**
>   **as we care for the least and the lost.**
Rejoice in this good news.

4

Thanksgiving and Communion

Offering Prayer (Matthew 25)

Mighty God, as we bring you our offerings,
    heal the brokenness we feel inside.
Turn our upturned gaze back to the earth—
    toward your needy children,
    toward the faces of those who hunger,
    toward the sick and imprisoned.
Turn our inward focus onto those in need—
    toward the lonely shut-in,
    toward the addict looking to get clean,
    toward the runaway hoping
        to return home,
    toward everyone society has left behind.
Only then may we truly see the face of Jesus.
Only then may we help heal our broken world. Amen.

Sending Forth

Benediction (Ecclesiastes 3, Matthew 25)

Every season in life is a blessing from God.
    We go forth, rejoicing in God's blessings.
Every purpose under heaven can lead us into life.
    We leave to bring about God's purposes.
Every act of kindness is a kindness done to Christ.
    **We go, determined to make a difference
    in our world.**

January 2, 2022

Epiphany of the Lord
Mary Petrina Boyd

Color

White

Scripture Readings

Isaiah 60:1-6; Psalm 72:1-7, 10-14; Ephesians 3:1-12;
Matthew 2:1-12

Theme Ideas

The magi sought a child who would be a king, but the palace was not home to this child. Instead, when the magi followed the star, they found the child in lowly estate, and were overwhelmed by joy. This is a story of pilgrimage, as we search for God's presence in our lives. This is a story of listening for the voice that draws us beyond the world's image of power. It is a story of the light that guides, us as God's true power overcomes oppression.

Invitation and Gathering

Centering Words (Matthew 2)

In the darkest night, a star shines. Follow this star, for it will lead to overwhelming joy.

Call to Worship (Isaiah 60

Arise, shine! Your light has come!
> **Glory to God in the highest.**
Darkness covers the earth,
> **but God's glory shines brightly.**
Lift up your eyes. Look around.
> **The light of God's love shines radiantly.**
Arise, shine! Your light has come!
> **Our hearts thrill and rejoice!**

Opening Prayer (Matthew 2)

God of light and love, shine upon our lives,
> as we welcome the mystery of your love.
Guide us toward your true gift,
> for our hearts long
>> to encounter with the holy.
Quiet our expectations,
> that we might be surprised
>> by the unexpected.
Open our eyes,
> that we might find you
>> in unanticipated places.
Shine your light upon us,
> that we might see you clearly,
>> and recognize your face
>>> in all people. Amen.

Proclamation and Response

Prayer of Confession (Psalm 72, Matthew 2)

The presents have been opened.
The cookies have been eaten.

The celebrations have left us exhausted.
Yet your Spirit comes again,
    guiding us toward true joy.
In all of our busy celebrations,
    remind us that you desire righteousness and justice
        for world in need of generous hearts.
May the light of Jesus Christ,
    the world's true light, live among us
        and turn our lives from oppressive power
            toward liberation and hope. Amen.

Words of Assurance (Psalm 72)

Like rain that falls upon the grass,
    like showers that water the earth,
    may righteousness and peace abound in our lives
    and in our world.

Passing the Peace of Christ (Isaiah 60)

The light of Christ be with you. The peace of God be
yours.

Response to the Word (Matthew 2)

When the travelers followed the world's wisdom,
    they came to the palace of Herod.
But joy was not there.
When the travelers followed the star,
    they came to the place of the child
    who was the world's hope.
There they were overwhelmed by joy.
Follow the star, which is the light of love;
    it will lead you to deepest joy.

Thanksgiving and Communion

Invitation to the Offering (Matthew 2)

The wise travelers brought their gifts to honor the promised child. Let us bring the gifts of our lives, in gratitude for God's bright light of love.

Offering Prayer (Matthew 2)

Giver of every gift, source of all goodness and light,
> we open the treasure chests of our hearts before you.

We offer you gifts of gold,
> to care for those in need.

We offer you gifts of love,
> to serve a suspicious world.

Bless our gifts and our lives,
> and use them to love and heal the world.

Amen.

Great Thanksgiving

The Lord be with you.
> **And also with you.**

Lift up your hearts.
> **We lift them up to the Lord.**

Let us give thanks to our God.
> **It is right to give our joyful thanks and praise.**

We thank you, creating God
> for the great light of your love.

When you called forth creation, you said,
> "Let there be light" and you saw that it was good.

You divided the light from darkness
> and created the sun, moon, and stars to light the sky.

It was good, as all your creation was good.

When your people suffered in bondage and oppression,
   you led them out of slavery.
You lit the way to freedom with a pillar of cloud by day
   and pillar of fire by night.
You gave them your commandments to light their way,
   as they strove to become a community of justice
   and righteousness.
When your people turned from your light,
   you were still faithful, loving them always.
You sent prophets to call them back
   to the world's true light.
And so, with your people on earth,
   and all the company of heaven,
   we sing your praises.
   Holy, holy, holy Lord, God of power and might,
   heaven and earth are full of your glory.
   Hosanna in the highest. Blessed is the one
   who comes in the name of the Lord.
   Hosanna in the highest.

You sent Jesus to us, the light of the world.
He promised that those who followed him
   would never walk in darkness,
   but would have the light of life.
The light of his life shone on all people,
   revealing the truth of your love.
He fed the hungry, cured the sick, ate with sinners,
   and proclaimed your truth.

Before he was betrayed, he gathered with his friends
   for a meal.
Taking the bread, he gave thanks to you and broke it.
He gave it to his friends, saying,
   "Take and eat. I am with you now and forever.

Let this meal feed you.
Remember me as you eat."
Then he took the cup, blessed it,
and shared it with his followers, saying,
"This is the cup of the new covenant,
given for the forgiveness of sins.
It is a gift for you and for all people.
It is my love offered for you.
Drink of this and remember me."

And so, as we remember Jesus, light of the world,
teacher, healer, guide, and friend;
we offer ourselves into Christ's service,
that we too might radiate God's light,
as we proclaim the mystery of faith.
Christ has died.
Christ is risen.
Christ will come again.

Pour out your Spirit upon these gifts of bread and cup,
that they may be for us
the living presence of Jesus Christ,
light of the world,
our hope for all creation.
Pour out your Spirit upon us,
that we may become the body of Christ,
as we serve creation
and reflect the light of your love.
Make us one with Jesus, and one with each other,
as we walk in the light, singing your praises.
Through Jesus Christ, light of the world,
and through the Holy Spirit, radiance divine,
all praise is yours, eternal God,
now and forever, world without end. Amen.

Sending Forth

Benediction (Matthew 2)

As you follow the star on your journey,
> don't look for the holy in places of power
> and prestige.

Instead, pay attention to the ordinary, the quiet places.

There, may you be overcome with joy,
> and share your gifts with creation.

January 9, 2022

Baptism of the Lord
B. J. Beu

Color

White

Scripture Readings

Isaiah 43:1-7; Psalm 29; Acts 8:14-17; Luke 3:15-17, 21-22

Theme Ideas

The power to protect and redeem Israel (Isaiah 43) is seen in new and vital ways, through the giving of the Holy Spirit (Acts 8 and Luke 3). The people God called by name, the people God accompanied through fire and water, have been given a new blessing—the power of God's very Spirit. This blessing is not just for the Jews, but for Samaritans and all who accept Jesus as the Messiah, the chosen one of God. With this blessing, however, comes judgment. The righteous will be gathered to God like wheat to the granary, but the unrighteous will go like chaff to unquenchable fire. The very power of God that brings peace (Psalm 29) is the same power that brings calamity on the unrighteous. These readings warn us against complacency and being cavalier about our baptism. The awesome power of God's Holy Spirit is nothing to toy with.

Invitation and Gathering

Centering Words (Luke 3)
The Spirit dances in the water, waiting in baptism to join us in the fire of God's love. Come to the waters. Come to the Spirit. Come to the journey of a lifetime—a journey through death to life everlasting.

Call to Worship (Psalm 29, Isaiah 43)
Sing praises to the Lord.
Sing of God's glory and strength.
   God calls us over the waters,
   and strengthens us for the journey.
Sing praises to Christ.
Sing of Christ's healing and love.
   The waters of our baptism cleanse us,
   renewing our spirits and nursing our wounds.
Sing praises to the Spirit.
Sing of the Spirit's comfort and hope.
   The flames of the Spirit are like a refiner's fire,
   purifying the soul to the glory of God.

Opening Prayer (Psalm 8, Matthew 25)
Source of love and mercy,
   as we enter a new year in the life of this church,
     may our love for you be made known
     in our love for one another.

Help us leave old grievances
    and former argument behind,
        as we open our hearts
            to the possibilities that lie before us.
Guide our footsteps into the glory of your ways,
    that we may live as you created us to be—
        beloved children, crowned with glory and honor.
May our worship reflect the greatness of our calling,
    and the honor of our heritage. Amen.

Proclamation and Response

Prayer of Yearning (Luke 3, Acts 8)

Divine Spirit, descend upon us this day,
    as you descended upon Jesus
        on the day of his baptism.
In the midst of our brokenness,
    we long to touch the healing of your Spirit,
        as you touch us with your love.
In the presence of evil all around us,
    we yearn to be protected by the holy fire
        of your sustaining Spirit.
As we remember, with gratitude, our baptism this day,
    remind us that we are a people of the water—
        a people made one and whole,
            through the Spirit made known
                in Christ Jesus. Amen.

Words of Assurance (Isaiah 43)

Do not worry, sisters and brothers,
    for God has redeemed you
    and called you by name.

Do not worry, children of the promise,
    for God is with us even now,
    gathering the lost into the light
    of everlasting love and faithfulness.

Passing the Peace of Christ (Matthew 25)
The one who baptized us with fire and the Holy Spirit is here to wash away our guilt and pain. Turn to one another and offer signs of the peace that only Christ can give.

Introduction to the Word (Luke 3)
Come to the word, seeking the presence
of the living God.
    We come seeking life with Christ
    in the promise of our baptism.
Come to the word, seeking forgiveness
for the hurts you have caused others.
    We come to offer our very selves
    as a living sacrifice.
Come to the word, seeking acceptance,
with hearts ready to be born anew.
    We come to receive God's Spirit.
Listen for the word of God.

Response to the Word (Luke 3)
People of God, do you know who you are?
    We are God's beloved children.
Disciples of Christ, do you know who you are?
    We are the wheat in Christ's granary.
Heirs of the Spirit, do you know who you are?
    We are works of the Spirit,
    fashioned into body of Christ.
Sealed in God's love, through the waters of our baptism,
let us abide in the power of the living God.

Thanksgiving and Communion

Offering Prayer (Psalm 29, Luke 3)

Mighty One, your voice is powerful,
     shaking the wilderness
          and stripping the forests bare.
Speak words of blessing upon our offering this day,
     that nothing may hinder the good our gifts may do
          in your name.
Give strength to your people,
     through the gifts we bring before you,
          that all may know the glory of your Spirit,
               through Christ Jesus, our Lord. Amen.

Sending Forth

Benediction (Isaiah 43)

Go forth and proclaim the good news:
God calls us by name
and fashions us for glory.
     We go as people washed clean
     in the waters of our baptism,
Go forth and live the good news:
the Holy Spirit blesses us
and seals us in God's love.
     We go as people blessed by God,
     that we might be a blessing to others.

January 16, 2022

Second Sunday after the Epiphany
Mary Scifres

Color

Green

Scripture Readings

Isaiah 62:1-5; Psalm 36:5-10; 1 Corinthians 12:1-11; John 2:1-11

Theme Ideas

God imparts the miracle of transformation in myriad ways: turning a jar of water into wine, imparting divine gifts to us, loving us with a steadfast love that never ends, rescuing us from exile, and restoring us with abundant love. The miracle of transformation flows through our lives, as it does through today's scripture readings.

Invitation and Gathering

Centering Words (John 2, Psalm 36)

Fill the emptiness of your lives with the abundant love of God. Then watch the miracles that follow.

Call to Worship (John 2, 1 Corinthians 12)

Come to the feast.

God welcomes us here.

Come to be fed.

Christ nourishes us with love.

Come to be transformed.

The Spirit re-creates us anew each day.

Opening Prayer (John 2, Psalm 36)

Living Water, flow through our worship.

Nourish us with your loving presence.

Draw us ever closer to you,

that our empty vessels may be filled,

and that our dry souls may be transformed

into fountains of love, life, and joy.

Proclamation and Response

Prayer of Confession (John 2, Isaiah 62)

When hope runs dry, lift us out of despair, O God,

and fill us with the waters of renewal.

When our efforts fall short,

forgive our failings,

and reclaim us with your promise.

When the weight of worry holds us down,

lift us up with your comfort,

and show us the way forward.

Transform our lives,

as you once transformed water into wine,

that we may flow with abundant love.

Transform your creation and your people,

as you once transformed a formless void

into this good and fruitful earth.

In hope and gratitude, we pray. Amen.

Words of Assurance (John 2, Psalm 36)

God's steadfast love shines as a fountain of light,
    transforming our lives with goodness and grace.
God does this as easily as Christ turned water into wine.

Introduction to the Word (1 Corinthians 12)

Listen for the Spirit to speak to our hearts.

Response to the Word (John 2)

Which jars are running empty in your life?
Where are you yearning for Christ
    to turn still waters into flowing wine?
Let us reflect silently together.
(Silent reflection and prayer)
Healing Christ, renew us this day.
Transform us into miracles of your love,
    that we may be the miracles
    you would have us be. Amen.

Thanksgiving and Communion

Invitation to the Offering (John 2)

Whether your jars are empty or full of wine, whether your gifts seem mighty or small, they are gifts to be treasured and shared, just as we are gifts to be treasured and shared. Let us share ourselves and our gifts with the world this day.

Offering Prayer (John 2)

Christ of miracles, transform the gifts we return to you,
    that they may be gifts of abundant life,
        and ever-flowing love,
            for a world thirsting for your grace.
In gratitude and joy, we pray. Amen.

Sending Forth

Benediction (John 2)

As we have been filled,
    go now to fill the world.
Fill the world with love.
Fill the world with hope.
Fill the world with Christ.
For as we nourish others,
    God transforms the world through us.

January 23, 2022

Third Sunday after the Epiphany
Deborah Sokolove

Color

Green

Scripture Readings

Nehemiah 8:1-3, 5-6, 8-10; Psalm 19;
1 Corinthians 12:12-31a; Luke 4:14-21

Theme Ideas

The passages from Nehemiah and Luke remind us that God's desire for all people includes release from all forms of captivity, whether literal or figurative. They also illustrate God's desire for restoration, wholeness, and healing. For Christians, this wholeness is not just understood individually, but communally as the body of Christ. As Paul puts it, "If one member suffers, all suffer together with it; if one member is honored, all rejoice together with it" (1 Cor 12:26 NRSV).

Invitation and Gathering

Centering Words (Psalm 19)

May the words of our mouths and the meditations of our hearts be pleasant to you, Holy One, our rock and our redeemer.

Call to Worship (Nehemiah 8, Psalm 19, Luke 4)

This day is holy to our God;
do not mourn or weep.
> **The Spirit of the Holy One is upon us**
> **to bring good news to the poor.**

This day is holy to our God;
for the joy of the Holy One is our strength.
> **God sends us to proclaim release to the captives,**
> **recovery of sight to the blind,**
> **and justice to the oppressed.**

On this day, may the scripture be fulfilled
in our hearing:
> **May the words of our mouths**
> **and the meditations of our hearts**
> **be pleasant to you, Holy One,**
> **our rock and our redeemer.**

Opening Prayer (Nehemiah 8, Psalm 19, Luke 4)

Holy maker of stars and planets,
   Holy mender of broken dreams,
      Holy fountain of joyful news,
         we stand in awe of your glory.
We cry out with the psalmist in wonder,
   as your word is proclaimed
      in the silent song of the cosmos.

We cry out with your faithful ones,
as your presence is made known
in the stories of your people
at all times and places.
When the people returned from captivity in Babylon,
you gave them your precepts to sustain them,
as they rebuilt the city.
When Jesus read the words of your prophets
to his hearers in the synagogue,
he reminded them of your promise
to release captives,
to restore sight to the blind,
and to free the oppressed.
Today, you call us to be members of the body of Christ,
your embodied Word made flesh,
and to offer healing and wholeness
wherever we go.
May our songs and our stories,
our praise and our thanks,
be pleasant to you this day, Holy One,
our rock and redeemer.

Proclamation and Response

Prayer of Confession (1 Corinthians 12)

Rock and redeemer, you call us to remember
that we are all members of one body in your Spirit.
Forgive us when we do not embody your love,
when we speak harshly to one another,
and when we judge others in our hearts.

Together, we drink of the one Spirit,
and share in the same love that makes us one.
> **Reclaim us when we refuse to hear your word**
> **when spoken by those who do not look or sound**
> **as we expect.**

Remind us that when one of your creatures suffers,
all of creation suffers.
> **Renew us when we forget that we are one body,**
> **one family of our heavenly creator.**

Words of Assurance (1 Corinthians 12)

Hear the good news:
> God heals our illusion of separateness
> and makes us one and whole.

In the name of Jesus Christ, you are forgiven.
> **In the name of Jesus Christ, you are forgiven.**
> **Glory to God. Amen.**

Passing the Peace of Christ (Luke 4)

Holy bringer of peace, help us embody your word to
one another, as we offer signs of peace.
The peace of Christ be with you.
> **The peace of Christ be with you always.**

Prayer of Preparation (Nehemiah 8)

Holy Maker, Holy Breath, Holy Teacher,
> as we prepare to hear your word,
>> help us receive the good news of your love.
>> with joy and delight.

Give us ears to hear it with the passion
> of the captives who returned from exile
>> in the time of Nehemiah. Amen.

Response to the Word (Nehemiah 8, 1 Corinthians 12, Luke 4)

Holy Keeper of Promises,
>we hear your word in ancient stories;
>we feel your Spirit moving in our midst today.

And we see you now in the members of your holy body
>who give thanks for the good news
>of your everlasting love. Amen.

Thanksgiving and Communion

Offering Prayer (1 Corinthians 12)

Holy Word, Holy Breath, Holy Maker of all,
>with gratitude for making us one body,
>>we share our gifts with one another
>>and with the world. Amen.

Great Thanksgiving

Christ be with you.
>**And also with you.**

Lift up your hearts.
>**We lift them up to God.**

Let us give our thanks to the Holy One.
>**It is right to give our thanks and praise.**

It is a right, good, and a joyful thing,
>always and everywhere
>to give our thanks to you,
>who used Ezra and Nehemiah
>to bring your holy word to the captives
>who returned from Babylon to Jerusalem.

You have promised that all who are captive
>shall be made free,
>that all who are broken will be made whole.

The heavens tell your glory in soundless song,
>sending your message of wonder and love
>to all people in every time and place.
And so, with your creatures on earth
>and all the heavenly chorus,
>we praise your name and join their unending hymn:
>**Holy, holy, holy Lord, God of power and might,**
>>**heaven and earth are full of your glory.**
>**Hosanna in the highest. Blessed is the one**
>>**who comes in the name of the Lord.**
>**Hosanna in the highest.**

Holy are you, and holy is your child, Jesus,
>who you sent to bring good news to the poor,
>to proclaim release to the captives
>and recovery of sight to the blind,
>to let the oppressed go free,
>and to proclaim the year of the your favor.

On the night in which he gave himself up for us,
>Jesus took bread, gave thanks to you,
>broke the bread, and gave it to his disciples, saying,
>"Take, eat; this is my body that is given for you.
>Do this in remembrance of me."
When the supper was over, he took the cup,
>gave thanks to you, gave it to his disciples, saying,
>"Drink from this, all of you;
>this is my blood of the new covenant,
>poured out for you and for many
>for the forgiveness of sins.
>Do this, as often as you drink it,
>in remembrance of me."

And so, in remembrance of your mighty acts
    in Jesus Christ, we proclaim the mystery of faith.
    Christ has died.
    Christ is risen.
    Christ will come again.
Pour out your Holy Spirit on us,
    and on these gifts of grain and grape,
        fruit of the earth and work of human hands.
Make them be for us the body and blood of Christ,
    that we may be the body of Christ to a world
        that awaits release from captivity.
Creator of all, light of the world, Spirit of truth,
    you are the one God to whom we offer our
        praise and thanks.
    Amen.

Sending Forth

Benediction (1 Corinthians 12)
As living members of the holy body of Christ,
    may we see the face of the Holy One
    in everyone we meet.
And may we hear God's holy word
    in every sound and voice we hear.
Go in peace to love and serve the world.
    Amen.

January 30, 2022

Fourth Sunday after the Epiphany
B. J. Beu

Color

Green

Scripture Readings

Jeremiah 1:4-10; Psalm 71:1-6; 1 Corinthians 13:1-13;
Luke 4:21-30

Theme Ideas

God knows us before we were even born. The psalmist proclaims that the God who took us from our mother's womb is our rock and our refuge. God promises
Jeremiah that he will be told what to say and how to
speak—for God puts words of prophecy in the mouths
of God's servants. Jesus knew only too well the effect
those words can have on communities, as his hometown
almost threw him off a cliff when they heard him speak.
And Paul warns that while God knows us and gives us
words to speak, we see only in part. What we share with
the world is only part of a much larger truth—a truth
that we will never fully understand until we see God
face-to-face. It is more important to love well than to

speak with the tongues of angels or to unfold all mysteries. This is sobering advice to those who eagerly proclaim the word of God while hiding the love of God.

Invitation and Gathering

Centering Words (Jeremiah 1, Psalm 71, 1 Corinthians 13)

God has known us, loved us, and been with us since before we were knit together in our mothers' wombs. Sink into the arms of Love this day, and trust the hand that holds you, for we have abided in this love long before we first drew breath.

Call to Worship (Psalm 71)

Offer God your worship and your praise.
Before God formed us in our mothers' wombs,
God knew and loved us.
Offer Christ your love and your devotion.
Before we drew our first breath,
Christ consecrated us as his own.
Offer the Spirit your gratitude and your thanksgiving.
Before we heard the call to heal the world,
the Spirit sustained our every heartbeat.
Praise God from whom all blessings flow.
We will offer God our worship and our praise.

Opening Prayer (Jeremiah 1, 1 Corinthians 13)

Wrap us in the arms of your love, Holy One,
for we need to feel your healing touch.
As we gather to worship you this day,
humble our hearts, teach us patience,
and touch us with kindness.

Open our eyes,
    that we may see ourselves as you see us.
Open our hearts to your Spirit of gentleness,
    that our words may be true
        and our love may be pure.
Bind us in a love that does not fail or fade,
    that we may bear all things, believe all things,
        and hopes all things in your love,
           which never ends. Amen.

Proclamation and Response

Prayer of Yearning (Jeremiah 1, 1 Corinthians 13)

Source of truth and love,
    we yearn for certainty in an uncertain world.
Grant us the courage to proclaim the words
    you place in our mouths.
Remind us that your love alone
    softens the heart and mind,
        allowing us to receive your mysterious ways.
When we fear that others will not see things our way,
    remind us that we all see in a mirror dimly.
Silence the clanging cymbals that distract us,
    and harken us to your voice once more,
        that we may abide in your love. Amen.

Words of Assurance (Jeremiah 1, Psalm 71, 1 Corinthians 13)

The one who formed us in our mothers' wombs
    continues to shape our lives today.
Rejoice in the good news:
    God knows us and loves us as we are.

God's love heals our wounds,
>   and gives us hope for the time before us.

Passing the Peace of Christ (1 Corinthians 13)
> We know that faith, hope, and love abide. Let us share
> this wondrous gift, as we pass the peace of Christ this
> day.

Introduction to the Word (1 Corinthians 13)
> With faith leading the way, with hope lighting our path,
>   and with love guiding us home;
>   let us open our hearts to hear the word of God.

Response to the Word (1 Corinthians 13)
> Love is patient.
>   **Love is kind.**
> Love is not envious.
>   **It is not boastful.**
> Love is not arrogant or rude.
>   **It does not insist on its own way.**
> Love does not rejoice in the wrong,
> but rejoices in the right.
>   **Love bears all things.**
> Believes all things.
>   **Hopes all things.**
> Endures all things.
>   **Love never ends.**
> God blesses us with this love,
> today and all days.
>   **Amen.**

Thanksgiving and Commuion

Offering Prayer (Jeremiah 1, Psalm 71, 1 Corinthians 13)

Source of every blessing,
you are our refuge and our strength.
Even before we were born,
you knew us completely.
You have watched over us
all the days of our lives.
Receive these offerings
and the gratitude of thankful hearts.
Grow the ministries of your church,
that we may bring your message of love
to a world deafened by clanging cymbals
and noisy gongs. Amen.

Sending Forth

Benediction (Jeremiah 1, 1 Corinthians 13)

God sends us forth with words of love on our lips.
Christ sends us with acts of love in our deeds.
The Spirit sends us with the power of love
to sustain our lives.
**We go in the power of God's love
to be ambassadors of Christ's love and peace.**

February 6, 2022

Fifth Sunday after the Epiphany
Michelle L. Torigian

Color

Green

Scripture Readings

Isaiah 6:1-8 (9-13); Psalm 138; 1 Corinthians 15:1-11;
Luke 5:1-11

Theme Ideas

Quite often, we feel inadequate to answer the call of
God. Just as Jesus is about to call Simon Peter as one of
his closest followers, Peter exclaims "Go away from me,
Lord, for I am a sinful man" (Luke 15:8 NRSV). Paul con-
fesses in 1 Corinthians 15: "I am the least of the apostles,
unfit to be called an apostle, because I persecuted the
church of God" (v. 9 NRSV). Similarly, Isaiah cried out
to God: "Woe is me! I am lost, for I am a man of unclean
lips, and I live among a people of unclean lips." After
grace has been given to Isaiah by a seraph, God asks,
"Whom shall I send, and who shall go for us?" to
which Isaiah responds, "Here I am; send me" (Isa 6:5, 8
NRSV). In this collection of scriptures, we sense that

God's call transcends our past actions and our shame. These texts nudge us to see our calling through the lens of God's grace.

Invitation and Gathering

Centering Words (Isaiah 6, Luke 5, 1 Corinthians 15)
In this season of light, God's grace has been given to strengthen and enlighten us. May our epiphanies and jolts of wisdom lead us to a path free from shame.

Call to Worship (Psalm 138, 1 Corinthians 15)
Great is the grace and glory of God.
We give thanks with hearts of joy.
Great is the strength and mercy of our creator.
We give thanks with hearts of hope.
Great is the courage and hope of our Lord.
We give thanks with hearts of faith.
Great is the mercy and compassion of the Holy One.
We give thanks with hearts of love.

Opening Prayer (Isaiah 6, Luke 5, 1 Corinthians 15)
Divine Deliverer of compassion,
> you call us to follow your voice.
"Whom shall I send?" you asked us.
With hearts of hope and souls filled with courage,
> we respond, "Here I am. Send me."
You evaporate our shame,
> and joyously embrace our authentic selves.
May we continue to open ourselves to you,
> and may we embrace our full humanity
> > as you do. Amen.

Proclamation and Response

Prayer of Confession (Luke 5, Isaiah 6)

Too often, we have clung to thoughts
   that we are too sinful for you.
Too often, we have fused our shameful pasts
   with a closed future.
From these beliefs, we condemn ourselves
   to an outlook without hope.
"Go away from me!" we exclaim like Peter.
"I am way too lost," we think like Isaiah.
But you have something different in mind.
You see us as so much more.
You see our divine image,
   and our creator-bestowed gifts.
Save us from our negative self-talk,
   that we may embrace your calling for our lives.
Amen.

Words of Assurance (1 Corinthians 15)

The grace of God has molded us throughout our lives
   and will continue to do so until our final breath.
God's grace is never in vain.
Even as God embraces our past,
   God moves us into the future—
      a future filled with hope,
      and the fulfillment of dreams.

Passing of the Peace of Christ (Luke 5)

Behold the children of God surrounding you. Through
your words and your smiles, acknowledge the spark of
the divine within them. See the presence of Christ in the
faces of your neighbors, affirming that we are all treasured children of God.

Response to the Word (Luke 5, 1 Corinthians 15, Isaiah 6)

Where might God be calling you?
> **Are you sure God is calling *me*?**

Find the grace that accompanies God's call.
> **With God's grace, we will journey together.**

Do not allow your past to stop you.
> **God's mercy will pave the way to the future.**

Thanksgiving and Communion

Invitation to the Offering (1 Corinthians 15)

The Divine Deliverer of compassion and care is calling us to serve, and to share our talents and treasures for the good of God's realm. No matter how we have fallen short in the past, God's grace assures us a variety of gifts to contribute. How is God calling us to share today?

Offering Prayer (Psalm 138)

Loving God, Deliverer of compassion,
> you call us to share our treasures and talents,
>> and the work of our hands.

With hearts filled with hope,
> we praise you for our bounty.

Forever shall we sing of your generous ways, Holy One.
Amen.

Communion Prayer (Isaiah 6, 1 Corinthians 15, Luke 5)

Shame has chained us, holding us back
from inclusive tables.
> **Shame has driven us from sanctuaries**
> **and gatherings.**

No longer. Guilt will not prevent us
from seeing God's grace.
In this space, all are welcome.
At this table, no lips are too unclean,
no hearts are too tarnished, no past too corrupt
to receive the gift of God's grace.

Great Thanksgiving

Through this table of bread and cup,
we look toward the future with hope.
We are reminded that our past lies behind us,
that the grace of God has overcome our fears
and our indiscretions.
Through Christ's great love,
we are no longer afraid of the future.
Through Christ's gracious meal,
we are provided a second chance.

Jesus loved his disciples through their imperfections.
Knowing they would desert him and betray him,
he still shared the bread and the cup.
"Remember me," said Jesus the Christ,
upon his blessings of cup and bread.

We recall the words and blessings of Jesus
each time we unite at his table.
We remember the gifts of Jesus the Christ
each time we wake to a new day
and step into his renewed future.

May the Spirit of God bless the great table of Christ.
May the Spirit of God help us recognize God's grace
in the breaking of the bread
and in the pouring of the cup.

May the Spirit of God encourage us
to embrace our divine callings,
as we all work to create God's realm here on earth.

Sending Forth

Benediction (Psalm 138, Isaiah 6, Luke 5, 1 Corinthians 15)

Fellow children of God:
Go forth, recognizing God's grace on your journey.
Go forth, discerning the Spirit's calling in your life.
Go forth, identifying the Christ as your guide.
In this season of light,
experience the steadfast love of God
and sing the ways of our merciful Creator.
Amen.

February 13, 2022

Sixth Sunday after the Epiphany

Mary Scifres

Color

Green

Scripture Readings

Jeremiah 17:5-10; Psalm 1; 1 Corinthians 15:12-20;
Luke 6:17-26

Theme Ideas

The paradox of faith often means that our lives are filled
with both blessings and curses, hope and despair, faith
and doubt, even goodness and evil. Placing our trust in
resurrection is muddied by our fear that death seems to
have the final word. The attempts to live goodness are
haunted by the sins and shortcomings of our lives. Even
so, God invites us onto the journey of life as partners
and cocreators. Even as God invites us to trust the journey, God reaches out to us in trust and faith. What a paradox to be trusted by God, whether we doubt or believe.

Invitation and Gathering

Centering Words (Luke 6, Psalm 1)

How fickle is the journey of life! Blessings walk alongside curses. Hope intertwines with despair. Goodness is shadowed by wickedness.

Call to Worship (Luke 6)

Poor or despairing, come to be blessed.

Hungry or tired, come to be restored.

Sorrowing or sighing, come to discover joy.

Bring your tired, your poor.

Share your hopes, your dreams.

Embrace your doubts, your fears.

Come as you are.

All are welcome here.

Opening Prayer (Luke 6, Psalm 1)

God of blessings and woes,

bless us with your presence this day.

Reveal your way forward,

and guide us in pathways of hope and grace.

In your blessed name, we pray. Amen.

Proclamation and Response

Prayer of Yearning (Luke 6, Psalm 1)

Shepherd of our souls, guide us through times of woe,

and help us find your solace and peace.

Forgive us in times of sin and sorrow,

and lead into your redeeming love.

Resurrect us in times of death and despair,
and lead into newness of life,
that we may be the blessing we seek
for everyone we meet. Amen.

Words of Assurance (Luke 6, Jeremiah 17)

Blessed are you who place your trust in God.
For the Holy One is faithful and true.
Christ's love is sufficient for your every need.

Passing the Peace of Christ (Luke 6)

As you have been blessed, turn to share Christ's blessings of peace and love with your neighbor.

Introduction to the Word (Psalm 1)

The word of God is a delight and a gift beyond price.
Come to be delighted, as we listen for God's word this day.

Response to the Word (Jeremiah 17)

Deep in our souls, God has planted roots
of faith, hope, and love.
Invite God to plant those roots so strongly within
that we might be like trees planted by water,
with streams of blessing flowing in and through us
to nourish others along the way.
(Silent prayer may follow.)

Thanksgiving and Communion

Offering Prayer (Luke 6)

Blessed God, with these gifts,
bring food to the hungry, hope to the despairing,
and comfort to the sorrowful.

Bless these gifts and our very lives,
    that we may be blessings of hope for your world.

Sending Forth

Benediction (Luke 6)
Go to bring blessings.
Go to be blessings.
    We go with joy, for we are blessed by God.

February 20, 2022

Seventh Sunday after the Epiphany
Joanne Reynolds

Color

Green

Scripture Readings

Genesis 45:3-11, 15; Psalm 37:1-11, 39-40;
1 Corinthians 15:35-38, 42-50; Luke 6:27-38

Theme Ideas

This Sunday focuses on dualities: lost and found, sin
and forgiveness (Genesis 45); the fate of the wicked
compared to the triumph of those who fear the Lord
(Psalm 37); the contrast between the physical and spiritual (1 Corinthians 15); and Jesus's description on who
and how to love (Luke 6). These scriptures present us
with choices that are always present—to choose God's
ways, or the ways of sin: anger, retribution, and enmity.
Jesus urges us to choose the way of light and love.

Invitation and Gathering

Centering Words (Isaiah 40:31 NRSV)

Those who wait for the Lord shall renew their strength,
    they shall mount up with wings like eagles,
  they shall run and not be weary,
    they shall walk and not be faint.

–Or–

Centering Words (Luke 6)

Love your enemies. Do good to those who hate you.
Bless those who curse you. Pray for those who persecute
you. Do this and you will truly be a follower of Christ.
(B. J. Beu)

Call to Worship (Luke 6)

God sets before us this day life and death,
blessings and curses.
    We will seek God's blessings.
Choose life, that you and your descendants may live.
    We will choose life.
Love the Lord your God,
and hold fast to God's holy ways.
    We will follow in the ways of our ancestors
    who abided in faith.
Come, let us worship.

–Or–

Call to Worship (Luke 6)

Come and learn the ways of life.
    We have come to follow Jesus.
Love your enemies,
and do good to those who hate you.

We have come to follow Jesus.
Bless those who curse you,
and pray for those who persecute you.
We have come to follow Jesus.
Do unto others as you would have them do unto you.
We have come to follow Jesus.
Come and learn the ways of life.
(B. J. Beu)

Opening Prayer

Loving God, we come before you today,
    seeking your blessings
        and your protection from the allure of sin.
Heal us with your love,
    that we might love one another.
Show us the truth we have found in Jesus.
Embolden our courage,
    that we may seize the opportunities
        you place before us.
Strengthen our resolve to spread your word and ways,
    and remind us that your guidance is always present
        through the power of your Holy Spirit. Amen

Proclamation and Response

Prayer of Confession

Holy One, Guardian of our souls,
    lead us into the light.
You alone know the secret places of our hearts,
    the dark places where we hide
        from your presence.

You alone understand our pride and envy,
 the strife we would pursue against others,
  our self-imposed limits of belief
   and faithful action.
We ask for your forgiveness.
Shine your light in our darkness,
 that we may see you more clearly
  and choose the light of your blessings,
   and the glory of your mercy and grace.
Amen.

–Or–

Prayer of Yearning (Psalm 37, Luke 6)

Teacher of hard truths,
 it is difficult to let go of our anger
  toward those who prosper through deceit
  and unscrupulous ways;
 it is not easy to make ourselves believe
  that the meek will inherit the earth,
   when they are being crushed
   by the powerful.
We long to see the vindication of the righteous
 and the prosperity of those who work selflessly
  to bring your realm here on earth.
We yearn for the day
 when all people will treat one another
  as they wish to be treated.
Help us live into that day, Holy One,
 even when it is difficult,
  that your love might shine like the sun
   through our lives and our ministries. Amen.
(B. J. Beu)

Words of Assurance

God forgives our iniquity,
and crowns us with steadfast love and mercy.
God removes our transgressions from us,
as far as the east is from the west.
Thanks be to God.

Invitation to the Word (Psalm 1)

Let us delight in the law of the Lord,
and meditate on God's teachings, day and night.
(B. J. Beu)

Response to the Word

We are pilgrim people,
traveling through sunlit meadows,
and darkened valleys.
But it is only when we dwell in the darkest valleys
that we truly see God's glory
shining on the peaks that enclose us.

–Or–

Response to the Word (Luke 6)

Be known as children of the Most High.
We will love our enemies,
and do good to those who hate us.
Be known as disciples of Christ.
We will bless those who curse us,
and pray for those who wrong us.
Be known as heirs of the Spirit.
We will be merciful,
even as our God is merciful.
(B. J. Beu)

Thanksgiving and Communion

Invitation to the Offering (Luke 6:38 NRSV)

Jesus said, "Give, and it will be given to you. A good measure, pressed down, shaken together, running over . . . for the measure you give will be the measure you get back." Now is the time to present our gifts and offerings to God with praise and thanks.

Offering Prayer

O God, your goodness and generosity
    are limitless and eternal.
We bring before you our gifts,
    as echoes of your generosity,
        that they may be used for good.
We know that it is more blessed to give
    than to receive.
May our giving be a sign of this blessing
    for others and for our course in faith.

Sending Forth

Benediction (Luke 6)

Go with God's blessings.
    As followers of Jesus,
    we will love our enemies
    and do good to those who hate us.
Go with God's blessings.
    As disciples of Christ,
    we will bless those who curse us
    and pray for those who persecute us.

Go with God's blessings.
>**As people of the Way,**
>**we will do unto others**
>**as we would have them do unto us.**
Go with God's blessings.
(B. J. Beu)

February 27, 2022

Transfiguration Sunday
Rebecca J. Kruger Gaudino

Color

White

Scripture Readings

Exodus 34:29-35; Psalm 99; 2 Corinthians 3:12–4:2;
Luke 9:28-43a

Theme Ideas

Moses has traveled through the desert with a people
who have just failed God by worshipping of a golden
calf, while Jesus prepares for a trip to Jerusalem where
he knows he will face execution. And yet, despite human betrayal, and because of divine presence, these two
men's faces shine: Moses's face radiates the glory of God,
Jesus's face radiates his own glory. We might expect the
disciples who see Jesus's transfiguration to shine like
Moses, but, no, they are afraid, confused, silent. They are
even powerless when confronted with a boy who needs
healing. Paul shows us where this story of fear and confusion ultimately leads: to people who will, because of
Jesus's radiant example of grit and love, be "transformed

. . . from one degree of glory to another" (2 Corinthians 3:18 NRSV).

Invitation and Gathering

(Prepare a loop of slides that can play through different parts of the service with pictures of high mountains and bright lights.)

Centering Words (Luke 9, 2 Corinthians 3)

See the glory of the Lord. Shine with the glory of God.

Call to Worship (Exodus 34, Psalm 99, Luke 9)

Mighty Ruler,
> **Most High,**

Lover of Justice,
> **Mystery Hidden in Cloud,**

Great King,
> **Forgiving God,**

Enthroned One,
> **Mountain Dweller;**

You are exalted over all people.
> **We praise your great and awesome name.**

We worship at your holy mountain.
> **For you, O God, are holy!**

Opening Prayer (Exodus 34, Psalm 99, Luke 9)

Holy God, bring us to your mountaintop.
We come to talk with you today.
We come to listen to what you have to say.
We come to sense your glory—
> a glory that can transform our lives.

May Jesus, your Son and your chosen one,
> and may the Spirit of freedom and glory,
> > shine upon us and cause us to shine like the sun.

Amen.

Proclamation and Response

Prayer of Confession (Exodus 34, Psalm 99, 2 Corinthians 3, Luke 9)

Mighty, tender, and forgiving God,
    talk of your radiant glory
        sometimes leaves us feeling lackluster.
We face daily challenges
    that can dull the shine of our lives.
When we figure these challenges out,
    we feel good at our success,
        but when we are unable,
            we feel unsure, afraid, and confused.
We sometimes wonder if we have the capacity
    to shine with your light
        in a world full of darkness.
Polish the mirror of our lives,
    that we might reflect your light more each day,
        even in times of fear and uncertainty. Amen.

Words of Assurance (Psalm 99, 2 Corinthians 3)

Our sovereign God answers our failings
    with forgiveness and renewal.
We are all being transformed, day by day,
    from one degree of glory to another.
Let us praise God's great and awesome name!

Passing the Peace of Christ (Psalm 99, Luke 9)

We are here today to worship God, whom we together praise and trust. We are the children of God, siblings in one big family. Out of the joy and hope of the faith that we share, let us greet one another with the peace of Christ.

Introduction to the Word (Psalm 99, Luke 9)

Jesus took three of his disciples with him up to a mountaintop to pray. While there, these disciples saw Jesus's glory, and they heard the very voice of God. Close your eyes and imagine yourself as a fourth disciple standing upon this mountain, as you hear the word of God.

Response to the Word (2 Corinthians 3, Luke 9)

(Prepare a small cutout of a paper mountain for each person. Also set up a mirror on each side of the sanctuary near the front "traffic" area. Above each mirror have a sign saying, "Seeing God's glory as if reflected in a mirror." After the sermon, invite people to write on their mountain [see below for the instructions]. Have them come forward and place these mountains on the communion table and walk past the mirrors as they return to their places. Have music in the background as people write. An easy song that doesn't require a hymnal can be sung while people walk. Some possibilities include "Turn Your Eyes upon Jesus" by Helen Lemmel, "O Lord, You're Beautiful" by Keith Green, and the Taizé chant, "The Lord Is My Light.")

Take a paper mountain and a pencil from the basket at the end of your row. Then think about one way you already reflect God's light and power in your life, and also one way you would like to better reflect God's light and power. In a moment, you will be invited forward and place your mountain in a basket. As you walk back to your seats, take a look in the mirror and see yourself, transforming from one degree to another with the glory of God.

Invitation to the Offering (Psalm 99, Luke 9, 2 Corinthians 3)

As individuals and as the church, one of the ways we shine in the world is by giving to others through our own skills and talents, as well as through our gifts of money. In so doing, we participate in the great plan of God to transform our world. So, let us give with joy, as we are able.

Offering Prayer (Luke 9, 2 Corinthians 3)

Jesus, Child of God, Chosen of God,
> you shone upon the mountain with your glory.

You shone in many other ways,
> as you healed the sick and fed the hungry.

You continue to shine today,
> every time we follow your loving example.

Bless our gifts of every kind—
> our energy and talent,
> our treasure and mission.

May your light shine through these gifts,
> that our world may be transformed by your power.

Amen.

Sending Forth

Benediction (2 Corinthians 3, Luke 9:35 NRSV)

Long ago, Jesus stood upon a mountain,
shining with the glory of his mystery and power.
> **A voice from a cloud rang out:**
> **"This is my Son, my Chosen. Listen to him."**

Listen for the voice of Jesus

> **We will listen and look for his glory,**
> **not only upon the mountains,**
> **but in our cities and in our homes.**

See it in your own transformation—
from fear to love, from confusion to trust,
from despair to hope.

> **We rejoice in the glory of Christ.**
> **We delight in one another, and in ourselves.**
> **Let us shine, shine, ever more shine! Amen.**

March 2, 2022

Ash Wednesday
Karin Ellis

Color

Purple

Scripture Readings

Joel 2:1-2, 12-17; Psalm 51:1-17; 2 Corinthians 5:20b–6:10;
Matthew 6:1-6, 16-21

Theme Ideas

Today marks the beginning of our Lenten journey. As
we walk with Jesus toward Jerusalem, we are invited
by the prophet Joel to gather as God's people. We are
invited by the psalmist to renew our hearts and to confess our wrongdoings before God. All this is done with
the assurance that God's grace fills our lives, and with
the promise that God's steadfast love never fails us. As
Matthew proclaims, when we give our hearts to God,
we discover the joy of knowing God, the joy of finding
our treasure.

Invitation and Gathering

Centering Words (Joel 2)

The invitation to renew our hearts is before us. The assurance of God's steadfast love is always with us.

Call to Worship (Psalm 51)

Praise God, who has taught us to sing.
Praise God, who has gathered us together.
We come before God to begin again,
to renew our hearts and our spirits.
Be assured that God's steadfast love
surrounds us and upholds us.
Thanks be to God!

Opening Prayer (Matthew 6)

On this day, merciful God,
we begin a journey of repentance,
a journey of renewal,
a journey of healing.
Sometimes this journey is hard.
We often don't know where we are going.
Help us remember that we follow in the footsteps
of your Son, Jesus,
our guide and guardian.
Help us be faithful on this day and all days.
In the name of Christ, we pray. Amen.

Proclamation and Response

Prayer of Confession (Joel 2, Matthew 6)

God of love and grace, we come to you
with our hearts wide open.

There are times when our hearts reject your love;
  times when we go against your ways;
  times when we display an unfaithful attitude.
Forgive us.
Remind us of your steadfast love
  and put a new spirit within us.
In your holy name, we pray. Amen.

Words of Assurance (Joel 2:13 NRSV)

The prophet Joel proclaims,
  "Return to the LORD, your God,
    for [God] is gracious and merciful,
  slow to anger, and abounding in steadfast love."
Brothers and sisters, siblings in Christ, rejoice,
  for you are forgiven and filled with God's love!
Amen.

Passing the Peace of Christ (Joel 2)

God has gathered us here, assembled as a faithful congregation. In the name of Christ, let us share peace with one another.

Prayer of Preparation (Matthew 6)

May our words be faithful.
  May our prayers be true.
And may our thoughts be guided by your Spirit,
  O God, our strength and our redeemer. Amen.

Response to the Word (Psalm 51, 2 Corinthians 5)

May these words fill our hearts
  and lead us to actions of faith

May we always remember the grace of God
that surrounds and fills our lives.

Thanksgiving

Invitation to the Offering (Matthew 6)
Knowing how much God has given us, let us come with
grateful hearts to offer our tithes and our gifts.

Offering Prayer (Matthew 6)
Abundant God, we bring these gifts to you
in thanksgiving and praise.
Bless these gifts,
that they may help your children everywhere.
As we offer you our hearts,
fill us with the treasure of your love and grace.
In the name of Christ, we pray. Amen.

Sending Forth

Benediction (2 Corinthians 5)
Go forth to begin again.
Go to walk this journey of faith with Jesus Christ,
knowing that God's grace goes with you.
Go in peace. Amen.

March 6, 2022

First Sunday in Lent
B. J. Beu

Color

Purple

Scripture Readings

Deuteronomy 26:1-11; Psalm 91:1-2, 9-16;
Romans 10:8b-13; Luke 4:1-13

Theme Ideas

Salvation comes from God. This theme runs through
each of today's readings. With a call to remember God
freeing the Hebrew people from bondage in Egypt, Deuteronomy records the fulfillment of God's promise to
bring Israel into the promised land. The psalmist rejoices
that God blesses the faithful with refuge and strength.
In Romans, Paul promises salvation to all who believe
in Christ Jesus with their hearts, and to all who profess this belief with their lips. In Luke, Jesus is tempted
by the devil after fasting in the wilderness, but resists
by putting God's priorities ahead of human calculations.

Invitation and Gathering

Centering Words (Deuteronomy 26, Psalm 91, Romans 10, Luke 4)

The one who led the Israelites into a land flowing with milk and honey, the one who ministered to Jesus in the wilderness, cares for us today in times of trial.

Call to Worship (Psalm 91)

When disasters strike, where can we go?
God is always there.
When enemies surround us, whom can we trust?
Christ is always with us.
When life is hard, who can ease the load?
The Spirit is always there to sustain us.
Come! Let us worship the God of our salvation.

Opening Prayer (Deuteronomy 26, Romans 10:13)

Faithful One, the promises you made to our ancestors
continue even to this day.
We too share the bounty of your blessings,
dwelling in a land flowing with milk and honey.
Burn the truth of Paul's words into our very souls:
"Everyone who calls on the name of the Lord
will be saved." Amen.

Proclamation and Response

Prayer of Yearning (Deuteronomy 26, Psalm 91, Luke 4)

Your ways, Merciful One, always lead to life.
When our faith falters,
and when we forget the promises you have made,
remind us of your steadfast love.

When our strength fails us in the wilderness of life,
  and when temptations threaten to lead us astray,
    remind us of Christ's faithfulness.
When our world seems imperiled
  by forces beyond our control,
    remind us that you are our refuge and strength.
In Christ's name, we pray for your presence,
  as we journey this Lenten journey with him
    all the way to the cross. Amen.

Words of Assurance (Romans 10)

All who call on the name of the Lord will be saved.
Trust the promises of God.
Believe in Christ Jesus with your whole heart.
Confess what the Spirit has done for you
  and you will abide in life everlasting.

Passing the Peace of Christ (Luke 4)

Jesus fasted for forty days in the desert while being tempted by the devil. At the end of this time of trial, he found the peace and strength to begin his ministry. Let us share signs of this peace, that we too may find the strength to sustain our ministries.

Introduction to the Word (Romans 10)

As you listen for the word of God, remember that everyone who calls on the name of the Lord will be saved.

Response to the Word (Romans 10)

Call on the name of the Lord and be saved.
  We will confess Jesus with our lips.
Believe in the name of the Lord and be saved.
  We will proclaim God with our words and deeds.

Live as faithful disciples and be saved.
**We will live the gospel in all that we say
and in all that we do.**

Thanksgiving and Communion

Offering Prayer (Deuteronomy 26)
Mighty God, you saved your people
    with terrifying displays of power,
        and with signs and wonders.
When your people were slaves in Egypt,
    you rescued them with a mighty hand
        and an outstretched arm.
In your never-failing faithfulness,
    you lead your beloved children
        into a land flowing with milk and honey.
We come to you today,
    thankful for your manifold blessings.
Receive these offerings as the first fruits
    of your bounty in our lives.
Send our gifts into a world
    that is hungry to know
        your refuge and your strength. Amen.

Sending Forth

Benediction (Psalm 91, Romans 10, Luke 4)
As you leave this place,
abide in the shadow of the Most High.
    God is our refuge and our strength.
As you wander through the wilderness,
put your trust in the Holy One.

Christ is our shelter in times of temptation and fear.
As you face times of trial,
call on the name of the Lord and be saved.
The Comforter leads us safely through.
Go with God's blessing.

March 13, 2022

Second Sunday in Lent
Deborah Sokolove

Color

Purple

Scripture Readings

Genesis 15:1-12, 17-18; Psalm 27; Philippians 3:17–4:1; Luke 13:31-35

Theme Ideas

Throughout the ages, God has promised to guide and protect those who do what is good, even when it seems that all is lost. Just as Jesus continued his healing work in Jerusalem, trusting in God despite Herod's threats to kill him, we too can trust God's promises, even when the road ahead seems full of pitfalls.

Invitation and Gathering

Centering Words (Psalm 27)

The Holy One is my light and my salvation; whom shall I fear?

Call to Worship (Psalm 27, Philippians 3–4)
The Holy One calls us to trust and pray.
> **God is our light and salvation,**
> **the stronghold of our lives.**

The Holy One calls us to take courage,
as we travel the path with Jesus.
> **Teach us your ways, O God,**
> **and lead us on our journeys.**

Blessed is the one who comes in the name of the Lord.
> **Behold the beauty of the Holy One,**
> **and bless God's holy name.**

Opening Prayer (Genesis 15, Philippians 3–4, Luke 13)
Lifegiving lover of all nations,
> you promised Abraham and Sarah
> > that their descendants would be more plentiful
> > than all the stars in the night sky.

You made a covenant to guide them
> throughout the ages.

Just as you guided our ancestors in faith,
> guide us here today,
> > and teach us your ways.

Help us remember the ancient stories,
> even as we place our trust in you
> > and exalt your name.

Bless us as we follow the path
> that leads us to the cross with Jesus. Amen.

Proclamation and Response

Prayer of Confession (Philippians 3–4, Luke 13)
Loving Guide and Protector of your children,
when Jesus began his walk toward Jerusalem,
he knew the journey could cost his life.

> **When we cannot see the road ahead,**
> **we are tempted to turn back**
> **instead of trusting the path**
> **you lay before our feet.**
> When Herod threatened to kill Jesus,
> he remained with the people,
> casting out demons and healing the afflicted.
> **When trouble comes, we are tempted**
> **to run away and protect ourselves,**
> **rather than remain with those who need our help.**
> Facing the cross, Jesus longed to gather the people
> as a hen gathers her brood beneath her wings.
> **Forgive us when we are not willing**
> **to take shelter in your loving arms.**

Words of Assurance (Psalm 27, Philippians 3–4)

> Hear the good news:
> The Holy One forgives and guides us,
> conforming us into the very image of Christ.
> In the name of Jesus Christ, you are forgiven.
> **In the name of Jesus Christ, you are forgiven.**
> **Glory to God. Amen.**

Passing the Peace of Christ (Psalm 27)

> As forgiven and beloved children, let us share signs of
> peace with one another.
> The peace of Christ be with you.
> **The peace of Christ be with you always.**

Response to the Word (Luke 13)

> Great, brooding Spirit of love,
> thank you for gathering us under your wings;
> thank you for showing us the way,
> and for holding us close to your heart.
> **Amen.**

Thanksgiving and Communion

Offering Prayer (Philippians 3–4)

Holy One, our light and our salvation,
   the stronghold of our lives,
      accept these gifts as a token of our commitment
      to walk in your ways. Amen.

Great Thanksgiving

Christ be with you.
   And also with you.
Lift up your hearts.
   We lift them up to God.
Let us give our thanks to the Holy One.
   It is right to give our thanks and praise.

It is a right, good, and a joyful thing,
   always and everywhere, to give our thanks to you,
   who brought Abraham and Sarah out of Ur,
   and who promised that their descendants
   would be as plentiful as the stars in the night sky.
The psalmist reminds us that you are a stronghold,
   a ready help in times of trouble,
   a caretaker of creation in times of need.

And so, with your creatures on earth
   and all the heavenly chorus,
   we praise your name
   and join their unending hymn:
   Holy, holy, holy Lord, God of power and might,
      heaven and earth are full of your glory.
   Hosanna in the highest. Blessed is the one
      who comes in the name of the Lord.
   Hosanna in the highest.

Holy are you, and holy is your child, Jesus,
    who continued to heal all who came to him,
    and yearned to protect the people of Jerusalem,
    even when Herod threatened to kill him.

On the night in which he gave himself up for us,
    Jesus took bread, broke it, saying,
    "Take, eat, all of you.
    This is my body, broken for you.
    Whenever you eat it,
    do so in remembrance of me."
After supper, he took the cup, saying,
    "This is the cup of the new covenant,
    poured out for the healing of the world.
    Whenever you drink it,
    do so in remembrance of me."

And so, in remembrance of your mighty acts
    in Jesus Christ, we proclaim the mystery of faith.
    Christ has died.
    Christ is risen.
    Christ will come again.

Pour out your Holy Spirit on us,
    and on these gifts of grain and grape,
        fruit of the earth and work of human hands.
Make them be for us the body and blood of Christ,
    that we may be the body of Christ
        to a world that groans awaiting your peace.
God of Abraham and Sarah, God of life and love,
    you are the one God, to whom we offer our praise
        and thanks.
    Amen.

Sending Forth

Benediction (Philippians 3–4)

Brothers and sisters, stand firm in Christ.
Trust God's promises in all things
    and take shelter in the Spirit's loving arms
    in times of trouble.
Go in peace, to love and serve the world.
    Amen.

March 20, 2022

Third Sunday in Lent
Kirsten Linford

Color

Purple

Scripture Readings

Isaiah 55:1-9; Psalm 63:1-8; 1 Corinthians 10:1-13;
Luke 13:1-9

Theme Ideas

These Lenten lections provide a number of reminders for the wilderness periods in our lives—times of struggle, illness, grief, loss, or simple ennui. Isaiah and the psalmist speak to the soul's longing for God's presence, for spiritual sustenance, for that which will truly satisfy. Both scriptures call us to seek the holy, to call upon God for mercy, love, in-filling, and help. Corinthians sets up something of a dichotomy between the body and the spirit, but this can be read at a deeper level—as an acknowledgement that even as we suffer, we can find strength in a faithful God who will show us the way through. Luke carries us further, encouraging us to take the suffering or the barren periods of our lives, learn from them, and use them to grow into newness of life.

Invitation and Gathering

Centering Words (Isaiah 55:1)

Everyone who thirsts, come to the waters. You who have no money, come, buy wine and milk without money, without price. Come, weary and worn, and God will fill your soul. For God brings blessing, even in the midst of pain.

Call to Worship (Psalm 63, Isaiah 55)

O God, my God, we seek you.
Our souls thirst for you.
Our spirits long for you,
for we are parched and weary
in these desert times, these wilderness places.
But your love, O God, is better even than life.
Our words will praise you,
our actions bless you.
Let us seek the Lord where God may be found.
Call upon the Holy One, who is near.
We will bless you as long as we live.
We will lift up our hands and call on your name.

Opening Prayer (Psalm 63)

Holy One, when we are alone in the desert,
wandering through the wilderness,
we call to you,
for you are our help.
Our souls cling to you.
Come, God, and hold us up.
Come, bring your presence
and fill us with your peace.
In the shadow of your wings,
we will sing for joy. Amen.

Proclamation and Response

Prayer of Confession (Isaiah 55, 1 Corinthians 10)

God of Mercy, we long to come when you call,
    yet often do not.
When we are most alone,
    we fail to turn to you.
When we are most afraid,
    we do not always think we can turn to you.
When we are lost, hurting, and in pain,
    we fail to realize how much we suffer.
We refuse to ask for help.
We lash out at others.
We numb our hearts.
We hide.
Forgive us.
But you, O God, are faithful.
You see us and know us and love us as we are.
In times of trial, you show us the way through.
Receive us once more,
    and have mercy on us.
As we seek your presence,
    help us place our trust in the grace of your heart,
        and help us begin again. Amen.

Words of Assurance (Isaiah 55, Luke 13)

Anything we have done, God knows already.
Anything we have hidden, God has already seen.
God's love for us and grace to us
    are higher than we have imagined,
    deeper than we have guessed.
Before we have asked,
    God's mercies are already given.

For God does not waste our struggles,
    but uses them to grow joy.

Passing the Peace of Christ (Isaiah 55, Luke 13)

Let us share Christ's peace with one another. For we are
called to feed one another as God has fed us. So shall
our lives bear fruit for all to share.

Prayer of Preparation (Psalm 19)

May the words of my mouth . . .
    and the meditations of our hearts
    be acceptable in your sight, O Lord,
    our strength and our redeemer. Amen.

Response to the Word (Luke 13)

Holy Brother, you never give up on us.
You remind us that our trials, our struggles,
    even our mistakes are not wasted.
When others believe there is nothing for us,
    you show us more than we could have imagined.
Plant your word and your grace in our hearts
    where it may be nurtured and grow.
By sunlight and shade, water and nourishment,
    may your word grow our lives
        in beauty and in truth.

Thanksgiving and Communion

Offering Prayer (Isaiah 55, Psalm 63)

God of grace, you have fed our spirits
    and nourished our souls.
You have supported us
    in every possible way.

May the gifts we bring this morning
    be an offering of our gratitude,
       and may they be a promise
           to share what we have received
             from your hand. Amen.

Sending Forth

Benediction (Isaiah 55)

People of God, listen that you may live.
Go forth and seek the Lord.
Find all that is holy wherever you go.
As our souls have been fed,
    so may we share our gifts
    and our blessings with others.

March 27, 2022

Fourth Sunday in Lent
B. J. Beu

Color

Purple

Scripture Readings

Joshua 5:9-12; Psalm 32; 2 Corinthians 5:16-21;
Luke 15:1-3, 11b-32

Theme Ideas

When the youngest son returns home in Luke's parable
of the prodigal son, the father tells his servant, "Get the
fatted calf and kill it, and let us eat and celebrate; for
this son of mine was dead and is alive again; he was
lost and is found!" (Luke 15:23-24a NRSV). Herein lies
a central insight of the gospel, indeed of all scripture:
there is something worse than death, and that is to be
lost; and there is something better than life, and that is
to be found. The prophets came to reconcile the chosen
people to God. Christ came to reconcile the whole world
to God. When we follow God faithfully, we eat from the
fat of the land. When we follow Christ faithfully, we are
a new creation—for we were lost, but now are found.

Invitation and Gathering

Centering Words (Luke 15)

The lost are found. The dead return to life. This is the Lord's doing; it is wondrous in our sight.

Call to Worship (2 Corinthians 5, Luke 15)

Like a loving Father,
God offers us freedom to choose our own path.
In God's freedom, we are a new creation.
Like a merciful Mother,
God offers us compassion when we lose our way.
In God's mercy, we are a new creation.
Like a forgiving Parent,
God welcomes us home with open arms.
In God's embrace, we are a new creation.
Come! Let us worship the one
who makes all things new.

Opening Prayer (Luke 15)

Merciful God, you seek the lost sheep of your pasture;
you call out to all who have strayed.
As the father welcomed the prodigal son home,
receive us back into your loving arms.
Your steadfast love, O God, knows no bounds.
Your loving embrace is always there for us.
Be with us in our time of worship,
that we may feel your presence
and know that you are our true home. Amen.

Proclamation and Response

Prayer of Yearning (Luke 15)

In your love, O God, we are never lost.
In your care, O Christ, we are ever found.
Help us feel this truth in our very bones,
for we are often far from home,
unsure of how to return.
Teach our shut-up hearts to embrace your hope.
Teach our shriveled souls to cry out to you.
For we long to taste the glory
of your heavenly banquet,
and we yearn to be held in your arms
as beloved children. Amen.

Words of Assurance (2 Corinthians 5:17 NRSV)

Hold fast to these words of assurance:
"If anyone is in Christ, there is a new creation;
everything old has passed away!"
In Christ, we are reconciled indeed,
for we have found our true home.

Passing the Peace of Christ (2 Corinthians 5, Luke 15)

In Christ, the lost are found and the dead return to life.
In Christ, we are a new creation. Let us celebrate our
inheritance and the joy of our homecoming, as we pass
the peace of Christ this day.

Introduction to the Word (2 Corinthians 5)

As you listen for the word of God, remember that everyone who is in Christ is a new creation, for everything
old has passed away. Let us be in Christ this day, as we
listen for the word of God.

Response to the Word (Psalm 32, Luke 15)

God is our hiding place,
　　our shelter during times of trouble.
When we come before God,
　　confessing our transgressions,
God receives us with open arms.
Why then do we tarry?
Now is the hour of our salvation,
　　for we were lost, but now are found;
　　we were dead, but now are alive with Christ.

Thanksgiving and Communion

Offering Prayer (Psalm 32)

God of overflowing abundance,
　　you bless the earth and it brings forth food.
We, who have been given so much,
　　rejoice in our ability to aid those who are in need.
As we present our offerings this day,
　　bless these gifts, the bounty of this good land,
　　　　that they may reach those who need it most.
May we, who call ourselves Christ's disciples,
　　continue to give freely of our worldly riches,
　　　　just as Christ gave freely of his heavenly riches.
Amen.

Sending Forth

Benediction (2 Corinthians 5, Luke 15)
In Christ, we are a new creation.
> **In Christ, we are made anew.**
In Christ, the lost are found,
> **In Christ, we find our true home.**
In Christ, those who were dead find new life.
> **In Christ, those who drank bitter dregs
> are invited to God's heavenly banquet.**
In Christ, we reside with the saints.

April 3, 2022

Fifth Sunday in Lent
James Dollins

Color

Purple

Scripture Readings

Isaiah 43:16-21; Psalm 126; Philippians 3:4b-14; John 12:1-8

Theme Ideas

The extravagant, even scandalous gift Mary gives Jesus, anointing his feet with perfume and her own hair, makes us wonder if we will give so much of ourselves to God. Our Lenten journey beckons us to be changed completely—as the psalmist's tears are turned to joy, and as Isaiah turns our gaze from the past to a new thing God is doing. Let us finally release burdens of injury and shame, that we may be free to give breathtaking gifts to others in Christ's name.

Invitation and Gathering

Centering Words (Isaiah 43, Psalm 126, John 12)

All you who journey with Jesus through Lent, trade your tears for joy, and your past for God's future. Give your best gifts freely to those who long for God's peace.

Call to Worship (Psalm 126)

When the Lord restored our fortunes,
we were like those who dream.
> **Then our mouths were filled with laughter,**
> **and our tongues were loosed with shouts of joy.**

Then they said among the nations,
"The Lord has done great things for them."
> **The Lord has done great things for us,**
> **and we are glad.**

Restore our fortunes, O God,
like ancient, flowing streams.
> **Let those who sow in tears**
> **reap with shouts of joy!**

Opening Prayer (Isaiah 43, Psalm 126, John 12)

Walk with us, Spirit of Christ,
on this Lenten journey.
Show us what to bring with us
and what to leave behind.
Give us the courage to leave the past behind,
that we may see the new things that lie ahead.
Then let us pick up our very best gifts
in order to give them to others in your name,
that our lives may be complete,
and our hearts may be made whole.
In the Spirit and the joy of Christ, our friend,
we pray. Amen.

Proclamation and Response

Prayer of Confession (Isaiah 43, Psalm 126)

God of grace, you call us into your glorious future.
When we dwell on the past,
     you tell us to remember no longer the things of old.
When we fail to notice the poor among us,
     you call us to give freely of what we have.
When we are reluctant to share our gifts and talents,
     you give your own life so that we may live.
Free us, Holy Spirit, from self-absorption
     and from fear. Amen.

Words of Assurance (John 12)

As God's children, forgiven and free,
     we are blessed to give our best gifts in God's name.

Response to the Word (John 12)

To give of ourselves completely is breathtaking.
To be generous is to be vulnerable,
     for we may fail or be judged by others.
But let us not live life in measured, hesitant giving.
Let us give all that God has blessed us with,
     even as Jesus gave his life so that we may live.
Amen.

Thanksgiving

Invitation to the Offering (Psalm 126, John 12)

The Spirit of Christ visits us in this place. Let us respond
by giving the best of our treasures and talents for the
work of God's church in the world.

Offering Prayer (John 12)

Receive, O God, all that we are:
> our treasures, our time, our talents,
>> and even our forgiven flaws.

May your grace be made known through our giving,
> that others may be healed by the Spirit of Christ,
>> our friend. Amen.

Sending Forth

Benediction (Isaiah 43, John 12)

May our service to others become a fragrant gift
> in God's name.

Go with God, the one who is about to do a new thing
> in and through us. Amen.

April 10, 2022

Palm/Passion Sunday
Bill Hoppe

Color

Purple

Palm Sunday Readings

Psalm 118:1-2, 19-29; Luke 19:28-40

Passion Sunday Readings

Isaiah 50:4-9a; Psalm 31:9-16; Philippians 2:5-11;
Luke 22:14–23:56

Theme Ideas

The king who is welcomed to Jerusalem with shouts of
praise and adulation will die horribly on a cross just a
few days later. Starting with Palm Sunday, and ending
with Good Friday, it's easy to view the events of Holy
Week as a journey from triumph to tragedy. Instead, the
opposite holds true. The triumph is in the tragedy itself,
as Paul reminds us: Jesus "humbled himself and became
obedient to the point of death—even death on a cross.

Therefore God also highly exalted him and gave him the name that is above every name" (Philippians 2:8-9 NRSV). Today, we take this same journey with Jesus, moving from delirious joy to abject sorrow, knowing that our tears will soon turn to surprised laughter. The best is yet to come.

Invitation and Gathering

Centering Words (Luke 19, 22–23)
Exaltation and joy. Passover sacrifice and betrayal. Death and life. Such is the terrain of Holy Week. Such are the waters that sweep us through the holy mystery of our faith—the waters that reveal the joy and the cost of discipleship.
(B. J. Beu)

Call to Worship (Luke 19)
Sing glory to God in the highest heaven.
> **The king is coming!**

Even if we keep silent,
the rocks will shout it out.
> **The king is coming!**

The king is coming!
> **Blessed is the one who comes**
> **in the name of the Lord.**

–Or–

Call to Worship (Luke 19)
Our king has come riding on a donkey.
> **Hosanna in the highest!**

Our savior has come to waving palms
and cheers of praise.
Shout alleluia!
Jesus has come to show us the greatness
of God's love.
Blessed is the one who comes
in the name of the Lord.
(B. J. Beu)

Opening Prayer (Isaiah 50; Luke 19, 22–23)

God, our help in ages past, our hope for years to come,
be with us in the joys and sorrows of life.
We turn to you this day,
knowing that we will not be put to shame.
Be at our side when the crowd shouts "Hosanna!"
as Jesus rode into Jerusalem.
Be with us also when the crowd turns,
as those who loved him fell away.
Their story is our story.
Be with us in the telling,
that we may walk with Jesus once more
on the long journey of Holy Week. Amen.
(B. J. Beu)

Proclamation and Response

Prayer of Confession (Psalm 31)

Lord, in your mercy, hear our prayer.
By your grace, help us,
for trouble is never far away.
We can't see or think clearly.
Our bodies waste away from grief and sorrow.

Our strength fails us.

Our misery is more than we can bear.

Yet even in the depth of our despair, Lord,
>   we place our trust in you.

You are our God,
>   our very help in times of trouble.

Let your face shine upon us and save us
>   in your unfailing and steadfast love! Amen.

Words of Assurance (Psalm 118)

All who call on the name of the Lord are answered.

There is nothing to fear.

The Lord stands beside you to help.

God's steadfast love endures forever.

This is the day that the Lord has made!

Rejoice and be glad.

Passing the Peace of Christ (Luke 19, 22–23)

The peace of Christ does not come from the excitement of parades with loud shouts of "Hosanna to the son of David!" The peace of Christ comes from resting in the promise of life in his name. Let us share this peace with one another.

(B. J. Beu)

Response to the Word (Psalm 118)

Give thanks to God. The Lord is good.

> **God's steadfast love endures forever.**

Declare it with thanksgiving.

> **God's steadfast love endures forever.**

The Lord is our salvation.

> **God has become our deliverer.**

Give thanks to God. The Lord is good.

> **God's steadfast love endures forever.**

Thanksgiving and Communion

Offering Prayer (Isaiah 50, Luke 22–23)

Jesus came as our king,
> to share your blessings with the world.

The one who was greatest among us
> became the least for us and our salvation.

Our servant king humbled himself
> to sustain our weary souls.

Receive the gifts we bring before you this day,
> that the whole world may know
>> the glory and power of your kingdom.

Blessed is the one who comes in the name of the Lord!

Invitation to Communion (Luke 22)

Lord Jesus, your hour has come.

You arrived as a king in the midst of a procession
> of waving palms and cheering crowds.

You moved among us as one who serves—
> an example for us to follow.

You have longed for us to join you:
> to eat and drink with you at your table.

Now your body is broken for us,
> like a loaf of bread.

Your cup is poured out for us
> in a covenant sealed by your blood.

We thank you for your amazing love,
> as we join you at your table—
> a foretaste of the heavenly banquet
> that awaits us in your kingdom.

Sending Forth

Benediction (Philippians 2, Isaiah 50)

May the same mind be in you that was in Christ Jesus:
>> the one who never turned back in defiance,
>> the one who gave his back to the lash,
>> the one who faced spitting and insult.

May your bearing be that of Christ Jesus:
>> the one who emptied himself,
>> the one who took the form of a servant,
>> the one who was raised to the heights
>> and given the name above all names.

May your lives declare the lordship of Jesus Christ,
>> to the glory of God. Amen

–Or–

Benediction (Luke 19, 22–23)

On the back of a donkey,
>> **Jesus came to bless us.**

With love in his heart,
>> **Jesus came to save us.**

From the power of death,
>> **Jesus came to free us.**

Go with the blessings of God's anointed.
(B. J. Beu)

April 14, 2022

Holy Thursday

Mary Petrina Boyd

Color

Purple

Scripture Readings

Exodus 12:1-4 (5-10), 11-14; Psalm 116:1-4, 12-19;
1 Corinthians 11:23-26; John 13:1-17, 31b-35

Theme Ideas

At his last meal with his disciples, Jesus washed their
feet, showing how they should serve the world. He
gave them the very essence of his teaching: to love one
another. He knew that his time with them was almost
over. That night, they shared a meal, and tonight, we
share that meal, as we remember the one who loves us.

Invitation and Gathering

Centering Words (John 13:34 NRSV)

We gather around the table, hungry for Christ's blessing.
He tells us, "Just as I have loved you, you also should
love one another."

Call to Worship (John 13)

We have traveled far, and our souls are dusty.
Jesus kneels before us and washes our feet.
How are we worthy of such love?
Jesus humbles himself as a servant.
How can this be?
Jesus fills us with his love.
What can we do?
Serve our neighbors with God's love.
(Sing "Jesu, Jesu")

Opening Prayer (John 13)

God of mystery, we gather tonight
    to remember the story that leads us into new life.
As Jesus washed his disciples' feet,
    may we learn to serve one another.
As we gather at the table,
    may we be ready for the journey ahead.
Remind us, O God, to love one another—
    even when doing so is difficult,
    even when we want to lash out in anger,
    even when we want to ignore those who need us.
We are not in charge.
We are called to serve, to share your love.
Be with us, O God, as we begin the journey
    that leads us to the cross. Amen.

Proclamation and Response

Prayer of Confession (Psalm 116)

In the midst of life's struggles,
we cry to you, O God.
Lord, save my life.

Save me, O God, from my selfish ways.
Lord, save my life.
Save me from my fears.
Lord, save my life.
Save me from my reluctance to forgive.
Lord, save my life.
Save me from my worries and concerns.
Lord, save my life.
Save me from my empty promises.
Lord, save my life.
Save me from all that keeps me from loving others.
Lord, save my life.

Words of Assurance (Psalm 116)

God hears our cries and supplications.
We are precious in God's sight.
We are saved by God's abundant love and mercy.

Response to the Word (Exodus 12, John 13)

Before the journey, God summons us to the feast.
This food sustains us,
even when we struggle and lose hope.
Let us be ready to follow,
trusting that God will lead us onward,
knowing that Jesus is with us always.
Let us serve one another in love.

Thanksgiving and Communion

Offering Prayer (John 13)

God of the ages, your Son told us to love one another.
Use the gifts we bring before you this day,
as expressions of this love.

Use us as your servants,
>   that we may care for others
>   through the ministries of this church
>   and through our very lives.
Use our offering to bring compassion and hope
>   to a world in need. Amen.

Great Thanksgiving (Exodus 12, 1 Corinthians 11, John 13)

The God of love be with you.
>   **And also with you.**
Come for the journey of faith.
>   **We are ready to follow.**
God beckons us into the future.
>   **Thanks be to God.**

God of love, you spoke the word,
>   and the world came to be.
Your breath rushed across the waters,
>   and the land and sea separated,
>   the sun, moon, and stars
>   danced into the heavens.
You summoned life of all kinds:
>   grasses and flowers, trees and shrubs,
>   orca and salmon, hawk and hummingbird,
>   chipmunk and giraffe, and people.
You proclaimed it good.
You declared the goodness of the earth,
>   and affirmed all creation to be radiant
>   with your presence and glory.

When Egypt enslaved your people,
>   you delivered them from bondage and captivity.

On the night before their long journey to freedom,
    you invited them to prepare a meal.
You told them to be ready to move,
    to eat the meal hurriedly, dressed for travel.
Then you led them out of captivity into freedom.
In the days and years that followed,
    your people were not always faithful.
Yet, you were always faithful, loving, and caring,
    showing the people how to live.
You sent leaders and prophets to call the people back,
    reminding them of your ways of love and justice.

And so with all your people on earth,
    we sing praise to you, God of life and love.
Holy, holy, holy Lord, God of power and might,
    heaven and earth are full of your glory.
Hosanna in the highest. Blessed is the one
    who comes in the name of the Lord.
Hosanna in the highest.

In the fulness of time you sent your Word,
    Jesus Christ, to live among us.
He fed the hungry, healed the sick, ate with sinners,
    and taught your message of love and forgiveness.
He knew that his life was soon to end,
    and gathered his friends for a meal.
He washed their feet and reminded them
    to serve others with compassion.
He told them to love one another always.

Jesus took a loaf of bread, and after giving thanks,
    he broke it and gave it to his disciples, saying,

"This is my body that is for you.
Do this in remembrance of me."
In the same way he took the cup also,
and gave it to them, saying,
"This cup is the new covenant in my blood.
Do this, as often as you drink it,
in remembrance of me."

And so, grateful for all your gifts in Jesus Christ,
we come to you, proclaiming the mystery of faith:
Christ has died.
Christ is risen.
Christ will come again.

Pour out your Spirit on these gifts of bread and wine.
May these things of the earth, wheat and grape,
feed us with the living presence of Jesus.
Pour out your Spirit upon us,
that we might become the body of Christ,
sharing Christ's love with all creation.
By your Spirit, unite us with Christ,
that we might go forth serving others
as he served us.
Let us feast at this meal
as we prepare to feast with Christ
at the end of time.
Through Christ, who showed us your love,
and through the church that journeys with him,
all praise and thanksgiving is yours,
loving and compassionate God,
now and forever. Amen.

Sending Forth

Benediction (John 13)

We leave this place knowing that tomorrow is
Good Friday.
Give us the courage to walk with Jesus to the cross.
Grant us the daring to see pain and suffering
in our world.
Even in times of betrayal and agony,
remind us to love one another.
We know that beyond the cross,
and beyond the tomb, there is hope.
Let us walk together with Jesus.

April 15, 2022

Good Friday
Rebecca J. Kruger Gaudino

Color

Black or none

Scripture Readings

Isaiah 52:13–53:12; Psalm 22; Hebrews 10:16-25;
John 18:1–19:42

Theme Ideas

Our two New Testament readings point to the rich
interplay of understandings that early Christians
considered as they pondered the crucifixion of Jesus
and its relationship to his followers' sense of liber-
ation from regret and failure to new life and hope.
Second Isaiah and the psalmist hold together the
same two seemingly incompatible realities: failure
and triumph, death and life. The fact that there are
so many images for these linked realities in these
passages implies the ultimate mystery of how God
brings hope from what seems like a dead end. Like a
cascading waterfall, these images of health, gardens,
sheep, and much more celebrate a God who enters

places of deepest suffering to find us and who then returns with us to healing and life.

Invitation and Gathering

Centering Words (Isaiah 52–53, Psalm 22)

I bring to you the dry ground in my life. I bring to you my troubles. O God, don't be far away! Come quick and help me!

Call to Worship (Psalm 22)

My God, my God, you are the Holy One!
You've been my God since I was in the womb.
You are the one who gave me life.
You do not hide your face from me.
You listen when I cry out for help.
You are the one who gives me life.
Let all who are suffering,
Let all who remember the sovereign,
worship, praise, and honor God,
the giver of life.

Opening Prayer (Psalm 22, Hebrews 10)

Strong Deliverer, Holy God,
we offer praise to you in this congregation,
because you have heard our cries,
you have remembered and answered us.
You have been our strength and our hope.
With confidence, we enter your holy presence,
remembering Jesus who led us to you
through the courageous power of his life
and the mystery of his death.

We draw near with true hearts
 bent on praising you and living for you,
  in the name of our brother,
   who carried the cross,
  and in the power of the Spirit,
   who rested upon him. Amen.

Proclamation and Response

Prayer of Confession (Psalm 22, Isaiah 52–53, John 18–19)

Forgiving God, we speak these words
 and sing these songs of faith
  with a confidence we do not always have.
We remember times when you answered our prayers,
 and we remember times when we felt alone,
  wondering if you even heard us.
We know what it is to feel sick in spirit,
 to follow our own inclinations
  and wander far away.
We are the very ones that Jesus came to find and help.
So we put ourselves in your hands,
 you who make all things whole.
God, the giver of life,
 Jesus, our savior and brother,
  and the Spirit that carried Jesus's breath
   back to God upon his death;
    we rest secure in your mighty love. Amen.

Words of Assurance (Hebrews 10)

My friends, Jesus opened up
 a new and living way to God.

Through him, we are cleansed from all regret
and wrongdoing.
Let us hold onto the confession of our hope,
for the God who promises healing and forgiveness
is reliable.

Passing the Peace of Christ (Isaiah 52-53, Psalm 22, John 18–19, Hebrews 10)

Brothers and sisters, our brother, Jesus, instructed us long ago to remember and celebrate his life, death, and resurrection—the mystery that makes us whole. Let us greet one another with the peace of Christ, who gives us this great gift of healing.

Introduction to the Word (Isaiah 52-53, John 18–19, Hebrews 10)

We gather today to remember a story that is at the heart of our faith—the story of Jesus's last night and day, the story that ends in his execution at the hands of political and religious leaders. Truly Jesus became the servant who was despised and crushed, who unjustly bore punishment. And yet the mystery of our faith is that his anguish leads to our hope, and the dry ground of his betrayal, crucifixion, and burial becomes the garden of our new life. Today we linger on the path of his suffering, and accompany him to his grave.

(Interweave parts of Isaiah 52–53 within the reading of John 18-19, like a repeated chorus to help interpret the John reading. Include Isaiah's reference to the servant as a young plant or root growing in dry ground, as well as John's references to gardens in John 18:1 and 19:41. Of the four Gospels, only John locates Jesus's betrayal, crucifixion, and burial in gardens. Try putting pots of bare earth in the worship area where people can clearly see them.)

Response to the Word (Isaiah 52–53, Psalm 22, John 18–19, Hebrews 10)

Jesus, servant of God and our savior,
    you grew up with little promise—
        a root out of dry ground.
In your life, you carried our illnesses,
    turning sickness to health.
You found us when we wandered astray
    like lost sheep.
You turned to us in our groans and afflictions.
And yet you descended to the dust of death—
    unjustly despised and tormented,
        while bearing the guilt of many—
            and were struck from the land of the living.
O Righteous One, our savior and ruler
    who was laid low in the earth of a garden,
        we stand in awe of you.
We kneel before you, waiting beside your tomb,
    knowing that God's plans for new life
        bear fruit through you, O Crucified One,
            who entered death to give us life. Amen.

Thanksgiving and Communion

Invitation to the Offering (Isaiah 52–53, Psalm 22, John 18–19, Hebrews 10)

Jesus did not turn from our suffering, but entered into it to clear a new way of hope for us. With our gifts and presence, we too may enter the suffering of others to share this way of hope. Let us give with Jesus's love for all.

Offering Prayer (Isaiah 52–53, Psalm 22, Hebrews 10)

> God of reliable promises,
>> you have faithfully turned to us in our need.
> Take our gifts of presence and treasure,
>> and use them to answer the needs of others.
> May those who long for renewed hope and promise
>> see your new life in the dry ground of their lives.
> For you do not despise our suffering,
>> but turn your face to us in love. Amen.

Sending Forth

Benediction (Isaiah 52–53, John 18–19)

> We stand by the cross of Jesus in wonder and dismay.
>> **We stand like the beloved few**
>> **who watched him die.**
> We remember the disciple who removed Jesus's body
> before sundown.
>> **We watch as the day becomes night**
>> **and the path leads to the grave.**
> We see the spices of myrrh and aloe,
> gifts of great love, as they are borne to the grave.
>> **We bear to the tomb our love, our fear,**
>> **our grief, our hope—gifts of our great love.**
> We begin the long waiting . . . through the night
> and into another day, and yet another night.
>> **We wait in night's darkness for the light**
>> **of God's dawn.**
> Go in peace and hope.

April 17, 2022

Easter Sunday
Karin Ellis

Color

White

Scripture Readings

Acts 10:34-43; Psalm 118:1-2, 14-24; 1 Corinthians 15:19-26; John 20:1-18 (or Luke 24:1-12)

Theme Ideas

It is Easter Sunday, a day to celebrate the risen Christ! The psalmist invites us to enter our worship space with glad songs telling of God's steadfast love. Acts and the epistle remind us that we are witnesses to an amazing story—a story of grace and hope, a story of Christ conquering death. John and Luke, while they tell the story a bit differently, move us from a place of darkness and uncertainty to one of hope, joy, and celebration. May we hear this story in a new way in order to share the risen Christ with the world.

Invitation and Gathering

Centering Words (John 20)

Christ is risen, bringing joy, hope, and the promise of new life. May this day be a celebration of God's abiding presence in our lives and in our world.

Call to Worship (Psalm 118, John 20)

Christ is risen!
Christ is risen indeed!
This is the day the Lord has made.
Let us rejoice and be glad in it!

Opening Prayer (Psalm 118, John 20)

God of new life and new possibilities,
    we gather to sing our songs of gladness
        and to share your steadfast love.
Some of us come from the shadows of our lives,
    as we anticipate the light.
Some of us come eager to learn,
    but are unsure of what it all means.
Some of us come in grief,
    grateful to discover hope.
Wherever we have come from,
    may we all find you, the risen Christ,
        the one who conquered death
            and proclaims new life for all.
In the name of the risen Christ, we pray. Amen.

Proclamation and Response

Prayer of Confession (John 20, Luke 24)

Holy One, we are tired and a little terrified.
We do not understand the confusing world around us.

It is easier to live in the darkness
     than to walk toward the light.
Forgive us.
Open our eyes to see your presence among us.
Open our hearts to perceive the risen Christ
     walking toward us.
Fill our hearts with amazement, wonder, and hope.
In your holy name, we pray. Amen.

Words of Assurance (Acts 10, Psalm 118, 1 Corinthians 15)

Brothers and sisters, siblings in Christ,
     we are witnesses to the resurrection story.
As witnesses, may we find hope in Christ
     and be assured of God's grace, forgiveness,
     and steadfast love. Amen.

Passing the Peace of Christ (John 20)

Christ knows our names and calls us with a voice of love
and grace. In the spirit of Christ, turn to one another and
share signs of peace.

Prayer of Preparation (Acts 10)

Risen Christ, the early disciples
     witnessed your acts of loving kindness
          and your ministry of peace.
As we hear your story anew,
     prepare our hearts to share the glory of Easter
          with the world. Amen.

Response to the Word (John 20)

May this powerful Easter story inspire us:
     to preach peace,

to comfort those who are weeping,
to help those who are lost,
and to proclaim our faith.
Christ is risen!
Christ is risen indeed!

Thanksgiving

Invitation to the Offering (Psalm 118, John 20)
The gift of God is here with us, for the presence of the risen Christ is with us always. In gratitude, may we offer our gifts, as we give thanks to the Lord, who is good. Truly, God's steadfast love endures forever.

Offering Prayer (John 20, Luke 24)
God of abundance, we offer these gifts to you
in thanksgiving and joy
for the presence of the living Christ.
May these gifts bring new life
to those both near and far.
And may we offer ourselves
in service to you and to one another. Amen.

Sending Forth

Benediction (Acts 10, John 20)
Christ is risen!
Go and preach the good news:
"I have seen the Lord!"
Go in peace. Amen.

April 24, 2022

Second Sunday of Easter

B. J. Beu

Color

White

Scripture Readings

Acts 5:27-32; Psalm 150; Revelation 1:4-8; John 20:19-31

Theme Ideas

Today's readings continue the great themes of Easter: resurrection, new life, and hope in the midst of profound fear and doubt. Revelation makes it clear that our hope is founded on the one who was, and is, and is to come: the Alpha and Omega. John affords a look at the role doubt plays in the life of faith. When doubting Thomas finds himself face-to-face with the risen Christ, he says, "My Lord and my God" (John 20:28 NRSV). Apathy, not doubt, is the opposite of faith. Doubt is an opportunity to dive deeper into our faith, and find our faith strengthened through the struggle.

Invitation and Gathering

Centering Words (John 20)

Do not fear your doubts. Mother Teresa, John of the Cross, and other spiritual giants were tormented by doubt during their lives. Doubt is a pathway to a deeper, richer faith—a faith where we can say with Thomas, "My Lord and my God!"

Call to Worship (Psalm 150)

Praise the Lord.
> **Praise God in the sanctuary.**
> **Worship God in the mighty firmament.**

Let everything that breathes praise the Lord.
> **Praise God with trumpet and horn.**
> **Worship God with lute and harp.**

Let the people of God sing their praise.
> **Praise God with tambourine and dance.**
> **Worship God with strings and pipes.**

Let the faithful join the strain.
> **Praise God with clashing cymbals.**
> **Praise God with beating drums.**

Praise the Lord!

Opening Prayer (Revelation 1)

Eternal God, who was and is and is to come,
> you are the Alpha and the Omega,
> > the beginning and end of all things.

Come to us now in visions and dreams,
> that our eyes may see more than they see,
> > and our hearts may love more than they love.

Make yourself known to us in this time of worship,
> for in you, we live and move and have our being.

Bring your kingdom here on earth,
>that all may know your glory
>>and find the courage to face each day.
We ask this in the name of the one
>who conquered the grave
>>to bring us eternal life. Amen.

Proclamation and Response

Prayer of Yearning (Acts 5, John 20:28)
God who abides in our doubts,
>we yearn for the courage to believe
>>where we have not seen;
>we long for the ability to perceive
>>things hidden from our eyes;
>we desire to embrace the riches of our faith
>>when death looms all around us.
Like Thomas before us,
>we often struggle to believe
>>the mystery of your resurrection.
So many doubts remain.
So much uncertainty closes our minds
>to the wisdom that stirs our souls.
Yet you work in and through our doubts,
>leading us ever deeper into the mystery of Christ,
>>through the power of your Holy Spirit.
May we see Christ's glory amidst our doubts
>and proclaim with Thomas,
>>"My Lord and my God!" Amen.

Words of Assurance (Revelation 1)
God has the power to heal us.
Christ has the love to save us.

The Spirit has the strength to free us.
These gifts are graciously given,
      even in the midst of our doubts.
God is here to lead us deeper,
      and show us the way home.

Passing the Peace (John 20:19)

Christ appeared among his disciples with words of greeting and support: "Peace be with you." Christ is with us now, offering these same words of greeting and comfort: "Peace be with you." Let us share signs of this peace with one another.

Response to the Word (Revelation 1, John 20)

The Alpha and the Omega works in our doubts,
      bringing us into a deeper relationship with God.
The beginning and the end of all things
      works in our weakness to transform simple faith
      into a deep and abiding awareness of God.
May our doubts be transformed into faith,
      and may our fears give way to courage,
      as we share Christ's good news with the world.

Thanksgiving and Communion

Invitation to the Offering (Acts 5)

Let us be generous in our giving, that others may see in us the transforming power of God. Let us be lavish in our gifts, that others may draw life from the bounty of God's blessings.

Offering Prayer (Revelation 1, John 20)

Alpha and Omega, beginning and end,
      you are the source of every blessing.

We behold your glory in the skies
    and touch your mystery all around us.
In the beauty of our awakening,
    our doubts give way to a deep and abiding joy.
In gratitude for your many mercies,
    we offer you these gifts and offerings,
        that they may be signs of our commitment
            to live as your faithful disciples. Amen.

Sending Forth

Benediction (John 20)
Believe where you have not seen.
    Our hearts will lead the way.
Trust where you have reason to doubt.
    Our souls will lead us home.
Hope where you have cause to despair.
    Our lives will know joy and peace.
Go with God's blessing.

May 1, 2022

Third Sunday of Easter
Mary Petrina Boyd

Color

White

Scripture Readings

Acts 9:1-6 (7-20); Psalm 30; Revelation 5:11-14;
John 21:1-19

Theme Ideas

We often think that we know what we should be doing.
We make our plans, and then the Holy breaks in and our
lives are transformed. An encounter with Jesus changed
Paul from one who persecuted the followers of Jesus
to one who proclaimed the gospel. Experienced fisher-
men found an abundance of fish when they heeded the
words of Jesus, who called them to leave their nets and
fish for people.

Invitation and Gathering

Centering Words (Acts 9, John 21)

We think we know what will happen and how things
will turn out. But then God's Spirit surprises us. Trust
the Spirit at work in you now.

Call to Worship (Psalm 30)

Sing praises to God, you people of faith.
We give thanks to God, who heals and restores.
Praise God who transforms us, who heals and loves us.
Praise God, who clothes us with joy.
Do not be silent. Praise the Lord!
We give thanks our God, today and always.

Opening Prayer (Acts 9)

Wisdom of God, come and dwell among us.
We gather to hear your word,
    and to sing your praise.
We come as we are, trusting that your grace
    will perfect us.
Interrupt our lives with your vision of truth and love.
We praise you now and always. Amen.

Proclamation and Response

Prayer of Confession (Acts 9, Psalm 30)

Loving God, we can be so sure
    that we know what is best.
We head into life following our own dreams.
Interrupt us with the blinding light of your grace,
    that we may gain new vision.
When despair and sadness overwhelm us,
    and when hope fails us,
        teach us to dance to the music of your love.
Open us up, O God,
    that we may see your path,
        walk in deeper faith,
            and be loving witnesses of your glory.
Amen.

Words of Assurance (Psalm 30)

Weeping may linger for the night,
>but joy comes in the morning.

God is at work, transforming our sorrow,
>giving us hope for a new day.

Prayer of Preparation (Acts 9, Psalm 30, John 21)

Interrupt our lives, O God.
Awaken us to your possibilities.
Surprise us and open our hearts to new directions.
Transform our hearts and minds,
>as we listen with anticipation for your word.

Amen.

Response to the Word (John 21:15-17)

Jesus asks, "Do you love me?"
>**Yes, Lord; you know that we love you.**

"Feed my lambs."
Jesus asks us again, "Do you love me?"
>**Yes, Lord; you know that we love you.**

"Tend my sheep."
Jesus asks a third time, "Do you love me?"
>**Yes, Lord; you know that we love you.**

"Feed my sheep."
>**We love you, Lord.**
>**We will feed your people with your love.**

–Or–

Response to the Word (Acts 9)

If God could turn a rabid persecutor
>into a powerful apostle,
>think what God might do with you.

You too are God's chosen instrument.

Thanksgiving and Communion

Offering Prayer (Revelation 5, John 21)

O God, you have power and wisdom and might.
You deserve honor and glory.
We come to you, Holy One,
> blessed by your abundant life,
>> to offer ourselves as your faithful workers.

We bring our gifts this day,
> trusting that they will serve your people. Amen.

Great Thanksgiving (Psalm 30, Revelation 5, John 21)

God be with you.
> **And also with you.**

Rejoice and be glad.
> **We praise God with joy.**

Thanks be to God.
> **We thank God with our whole hearts.**

We join with every creature in heaven and on earth,
> every creature under the earth and in the sea,
> to sing your praises.

You created all that is, bringing forth goodness
> and new life.

You are at work in our world still,
> transforming lives, healing brokenness,
> comforting those who mourn.

Your people were not always faithful.
They followed their own desires, lashing out in anger,
> forgetting those in need.

You sent prophets to call them back to your paths,
> reminding them of your love,
> and telling them to care for one another.

You were always faithful, for you loved your people.

And so, we join all creation as we sing praise to you:
Worthy is our God and worthy is Jesus Christ!
Power and might be yours!
Wisdom and honor be yours!
Glory and blessing be yours!
Amen and amen. Now and forever. Amen.

You gave us Jesus to walk with us
and to show us your love.
He healed the sick, fed the hungry,
and taught us your ways.
He showed us the abundance of your love
and reminded us to share it with others.

On the night before his death,
Jesus gathered with his followers,
telling them to love one another.
He shared a meal with them, taking bread, blessing it,
breaking it, and giving it to them, saying,
"This is my very being. When you eat this,
remember that I am with you."
He took the cup, blessed it, and gave it, saying,
"This is the cup of forgiveness,
poured out in abundance for you and for all people.
As you drink this, remember that I am with you."

And so, we offer our very selves,
with glad and grateful hearts,
as we proclaim this mystery:
Christ was with us from the beginning.
Christ is with us today.
Christ will be with us until the end of time.

Send your spirit of abundant love
upon these gifts of the earth,
bread and wine.

Transform them, by the power of your grace,
    into food for our bodies
        and nourishment for our souls.
Send your Spirit upon us,
    and transform us by the power of your Wisdom,
        that we may become the body of Christ,
            feeding his lambs, and tending to his sheep.
All praise is yours, God of power and might,
    wisdom and honor, glory and blessing.
All praise is yours, now and forever.
    Amen.

Sending Forth

Benediction (John 21)
Go forth to feed and tend God's people.
Do so because you love Jesus,
    and because Jesus loves and needs you.
May the abundant blessings of God's love
    surround and feed you,
        as God renews you day by day.

May 8, 2022

Fourth Sunday of Easter
Festival of the Christian Home/Mother's Day
B. J. Beu

Color

White

Scripture Readings

Acts 9:36-43; Psalm 23; Revelation 7:9-17; John 10:22-30

Theme Ideas

The resurrected Christ is our one true shepherd—the good shepherd spoken of by the psalmist, who leads God's flock through fear and trials to rest beside still waters. Christ is the shepherd spoken of in John's Gospel and in the book of Revelation—the one who leads God's flock to springs of eternal life, and who wipes away every tear. Christ is our shepherd, and when we hear and follow the call of our shepherd, we belong to God's flock. No one can snatch us from God's hand.

Invitation and Gathering

Centering Words (John 10)

Christ is our shepherd, who knows us and calls us. Our shepherd gives us eternal life; no one can snatch us from his hand.

Call to Worship (Psalm 23, John 10)

Christ is our shepherd.
> **We are Christ's sheep.**

The shepherd is calling us to join God's flock.
> **We will follow our shepherd.**

Rejoice, little one, for no one can snatch us
from the shepherd's hand.
> **In God's flock, we rest secure.**

Come! Let us worship.

Opening Prayer (Acts 9, Revelation 7)

Loving Shepherd, in the midst of sorrow and loss,
> you wipe away every tear from our eyes.

May the wonders of your love
> reach down to us this day.

As Peter raised Tabitha from the dead,
> raise us also to new life.

Help us cling no longer to the darkness
> threatening to overcome our world,
>> that we may reside in the glory of the Lamb.

Wake us from the slumber that numbs our spirit,
> even as you nourish us in the strength of your Spirit.

May the world see the shepherd living in us,
> and may we come to dwell in your pastures,
>> which remain ever green. Amen.

Proclamation and Response

Prayer of Yearning (Revelation 7:10 NRSV)

The voices of your faithful ones echo in our ears:
"Salvation belongs to our God
who is seated on the throne,
and to the Lamb!"
We long to join their words of praise,
but feel unworthy.
We know that you are our shepherd,
watching over us every minute of our lives.
We yearn to join the chorus
of those worshipping the Lamb,
but we feel unsure and insecure.
Open us to the one who wipes away every tear,
that we may truly rest in green pastures
and drink from still waters.
For you alone restore our souls.
You alone meet us in our time of need. Amen.

Words of Assurance (John 10:27-28 NRSV)

Trust the words of our shepherd:
"My sheep hear my voice.
I know them, and they follow me.
I give them eternal life, and they will never perish.
No one will snatch them out of my hand."
Rest secure that our shepherd loves us,
and leads us into life.

Passing the Peace (John 20)

We rest secure in God's flock. In gratitude and thanks,
let us share signs of peace from our shepherd, who
watches over us.

Response to the Word (Psalm 23, Revelation 7)

The good shepherd calls to us.
We will follow our shepherd.
Drink deeply from the springs of eternal life.
We have tasted it's sweet waters.
Rest secure, for our shepherd watches over us.
The good shepherd wipes away our tears.
With our shepherd, we can live unafraid.

Thanksgiving and Communion

Offering Prayer (Acts 9)

Loving Shepherd, we thank you for your tender care.
Everything we have comes the goodness of your love.
Receive the gifts we return to you now,
    that sheep in other flocks may come to know you
      and discover that you are the one
        who lays down your life for the flock. Amen.

Sending Forth

Benediction (Psalm 23)

The Lord is our shepherd; we shall not want.
We lie down in green pastures
and drink from still waters.
Our shepherd restores our souls.
Even though we walk through the darkest valleys,
we fear no evil, for our shepherd travels with us.
Surely goodness and mercy shall follow us
all the days of our lives.
And we will dwell in with our shepherd forever.

May 15, 2022

Fifth Sunday of Easter
Mark Sorensen

Color

White

Scripture Readings

Acts 11:1-18; Psalm 148; Revelation 21:1-6; John 13:31-35

Theme Ideas

What demands our worship? More significantly, what is truly worthy of our worship? Today's scriptures speak to these questions. They speak of the kind of worship that is big; the kind of worship that is loud; the kind of worship that, when it flows from the heart, spills out into our relationships with everyone we meet. God dwells among us. Right here, right now. Today's scriptures bring us into the presence of the one who is truly worthy of our praise and adoration.

Invitation and Gathering

Centering Words (Revelation 21)

Each morning we awake to a blank canvass. Our God makes all things new!

Call to Worship (Psalm 148, Revelation 21)

As the sun rises in the morning,
let all creation worship God.
From the highest mountains to the deepest seas,
let all creation proclaim the name of the Lord,
for God alone is worthy to be praised.
God alone makes all things new.
All praise, glory, and honor be yours, forever.

Opening Prayer (Acts 11, Psalm 148)

Gracious and loving God,
you meet us where we are.
We gather together from many walks of life,
but we are unified as one heart
in the body of Christ.
In our time of worship,
open our ears to hear your voice;
open our eyes to see your glory;
open our minds to receive your word;
open our hearts to perceive your presence.
Amen.

Proclamation and Response

Prayer of Confession (Psalm 148, John 13)

Eternal God, it's so easy to get lost
in the noise and busyness of life.
Forgive the times we lose focus
and forget the praise we owe you,
offering it to the world instead.
You alone are worthy of our praise.
You alone are worthy of our adoration.

You alone are worthy of our love.
Creator who makes all things new,
 renew our hearts and strengthen our resolve,
  that we may graciously receive
   what you have in store for us today.

Words of Assurance (Revelation 21)

When we are thirsty, God renews our souls
 with living waters.
Drink deeply, knowing that in Jesus Christ,
 we are forgiven.

Passing the Peace of Christ (John 13)

Jesus commands us to love one another. Take a moment
and turn to your neighbor, sharing the same love God
has so richly bestowed upon each of us.

Response to the Word (Acts 11)

Loving and gracious God,
 we turn to you in our need.
Help us be a community
 that looks to you for guidance.
Help us be a people
 that turns to you for the tasks
  you would have us do.
Help us be a church
 that looks to you for understanding and wisdom.
Help us be a community
 that knows the power of your Holy Spirit.

Thanksgiving and Communion

Offering Prayer (Psalm 148, Revelation 21)

Holy God, you have given us so much.
Through your love and abundance,
   our cup overflows.
From the bounty of your blessings,
   we offer these gifts back to you.
Use these offerings for your glory,
   as we work to bring your kingdom here on earth.
Amen.

Sending Forth

Benediction (John 13)

As you leave this place,
   know that our worship is only beginning.
Go to love others as God has first loved us.
In all that we see, hear, and take into our hearts,
   may the love of Christ be with us,
   now and forevermore. Amen.

May 22, 2022

Sixth Sunday of Easter
Catarina Paton

Color

White

Scripture Readings

Acts 16:9-15; Psalm 67; Revelation 21:1-10, 22–22:5; John 14:23-29

Theme Ideas

All four scriptures share a sense that God is with us no matter where we may be in our lives. Psalm 67 and Revelation show us God's blessings, but warn that these blessings can be taken from us if we go astray. John and Acts show us that we are welcomed in God's kingdom, as were our ancestors before us, and as generations will that come after us.

Invitation and Gathering

Centering Words (John 14)

Those who devote their love to God receive unending love and devotion.

Call to Worship (Psalm 67, Revelation 21, John 14)

Jesus dwells among us,
teaching us to believe in his name.
Let us offer God our thanks.
The Holy Spirit dwells among us,
guiding us down the paths of life.
Let us offer God our praise.
God dwells among us,
beckoning us to worship.
Let us offer God our worship.

Opening Prayer (Acts 16, John 14)

Loving companion, you give your people visions,
allowing us to believe in your words.
We come to you today
to keep our word, profess our love,
and proclaim our faith.
Nurture our hearts with your teachings,
and nurture our minds with your grace. Amen.

Proclamation and Response

Prayer of Confession (Revelation 21, Psalm 67)

Father, Abba, like generations before us,
we have failed to keep your word
and live in your ways.
Your glory shines a light on our humanness
and our ability to be faithless.
Under the lights of your holy city,
illuminate the path to your heavenly throne.

Guide us by your Spirit,
that we may receive the life-giving waters
that flows from your heavenly home.

Words of Assurance (John 14)

Holy One, you have left your peace with us,
that we may hear you and never become troubled
by the world around us.

Passing the Peace of Christ (Psalm 67)

We have been blessed by the grace of God's goodness—a
grace that allows the fair judgment of us all. May we
offer up our own blessings, as we exchange signs of
Christ's peace with one another this morning.

Response to the Word (Acts 16)

Like families of faith who came before us,
we open our hearts and houses to your message.
Your visions and words proclaim the good news
you have to share with us.

Thanksgiving and Communion

Invitation to the Offering (Acts 16, Revelation 21, Psalm 67)

Our lives have been blessed by flowing waters
and harvests of fruits.
Let us share our harvests with you and your world.

Offering Prayer (Revelation 21, John 14)

Creator and almighty God, from city to city,
you continue to bless our lives.
Wherever we find ourselves,
the bounty of your peace meets us there.

We bring these gifts to you
in order to share our bounty,
as you have shared yours with us.
May those who need these gifts find your presence,
even as they receive what they need.
May their paths of faith be lit with your light,
as ours have been.
In your holy name, we pray. Amen

Sending Forth

Benediction (Acts 21, Psalm 67)
God has a dwelling place with you.
You have a dwelling place in Christ,
a source of continual blessing in your life.
Go forth to spread God's message,
that others may also dwell in peace.

May 29, 2022

Ascension Sunday

B. J. Beu

Color

White

Scripture Readings

Acts 1:1-11; Psalm 47; Ephesians 1:15-23; Luke 24:44-53

Alternate Scripture Readings for Seventh Sunday of Easter

Acts 16:16-34; Psalm 97; Revelation 22:12-14, 16-17, 20-21; John 17:20-26

Theme Ideas

Ascension Sunday is about a power that lies beyond our ordinary existence. Through the same power that raised Jesus from the dead the same power that heals our bodies and our souls, we receive the gifts of the Holy Spirit. As Jesus is lifted up to the heavens, we are reminded to look beyond earthly power to the power of the Most High.

Invitation and Gathering

Centering Words (Acts 1, Luke 24)

Wait to be clothed with power from on high. The one who ascended will come to us again, bringing new life and new hope.

Call to Worship (Psalm 47)

Clap your hands, people of God.
   Shout to God with cries of joy.
Look to the heavens, brothers and sisters in Christ.
   Witness the power of our God.
Clap your hands, people of God.
   Shout to God with cries of joy.

Opening Prayer (Acts 1, Luke 24)

God of mystery, part the veil
      that keeps us from seeing
         your full glory and might.
Open our eyes to behold the risen Christ,
      who ascended to you in glory.
Open our hearts this day,
      that our spirits may ascend to you
         as he ascended that day.
Focus our thoughts on the power of your salvation,
      that we may move beyond the mundane
         to contemplate mysteries and wonders
            worthy of our meditations.
May we be found worthy of your great gifts,
      and may we be clothed with your power on high.
Amen.

Proclamation and Response

Prayer of Yearning (Acts 1, Ephesians 1, Luke 24)

Merciful God, raise our sights and our hopes.
Even as we yearn for your glorious inheritance,
    we settle for so much less.
Even as we long to behold the extraordinary,
    we keep our eyes fixed on the ground.
Even as we hope to inherit your glorious kingdom,
    we keep our hearts attuned to earthly power.
Even as we desire to rest in the arms of your love,
    we listen to voices that sow discord.
May your Holy Spirit find us ready
    when the one who ascended on high
        returns to his own. Amen.

Words of Assurance (Acts 1, Ephesians 1, Luke 24)

Wait patiently for the Spirit to stir your spirit.
Wait hopefully to be filled by the living God.
For God justifies our hope,
    and Christ fills our cup with power from on high.

Passing the Peace (Ephesians 1)

Christ offers his glorious inheritance among the saints.
Rest in this blessed assurance, as we share signs of the
peace of Christ with one another.

Response to the Word (Ephesians 1)

Having heard the word,
    may God enlighten you with wisdom.
As you ponder God's word in your heart,
    may Christ bless you with the hope
    to which you have been called.

And as you live these words each and every day,
may you know the greatness of God's power
and our glorious inheritance among the saints.

Thanksgiving and Communion

Offering Prayer (Psalm 47)

Your power and might, O God,
bring forth our worship and praise.
Your love and mercy, Compassionate One,
call forth our gratefulness and thanksgiving.
In appreciation for your blessing in our lives,
we offer you these gifts from our hearts,
this fruit of our industry.
Receive them, we pray,
in the name of the one who ascended to heaven,
that our lives here on earth
might be filled with your Spirit. Amen.

Sending Forth

Benediction (Luke 24)

Lift up your eyes to the heavens.
Christ ascended to show us the way.
Trust the Spirit's power.
Christ ascended to clothe us with power.
Go as witnesses of the risen Lord.
Christ ascended to bring us eternal life.

June 5, 2022

Pentecost Sunday
Deborah Sokolove

Color

Red

Scripture Readings

Acts 2:1-21; Psalm 104:24-34, 35b; Romans 8:14-17; John 14:8-17 (25-27)

Theme Ideas

Following the death and resurrection of Jesus, his disciples were often confused and afraid, even though he had promised that they would not be left alone after his death. The day of Pentecost celebrates the ways that the Holy Spirit acts within all who believe, helping us let go of fear, dream of a better future, and trust God in all things.

Invitation and Gathering

Centering Words (John 14)

Do not let your hearts be troubled, and do not let them be afraid.

Call to Worship (Acts 2)

The Holy One calls our sons and our daughters
to prophesy.
> **We come, ready to hear the word of God.**
The Holy One calls our young people to see visions.
> **We come, ready to see new visions.**
The Holy One calls our elders to dream dreams.
> **We come, ready to dream new dreams.**
The Spirit of the Holy One is poured upon all flesh.
> **We come, ready to be filled with God's Spirit.**

Opening Prayer (Acts 2, John 14)

God of breath and fire, God of past and future,
God of all that is and all that ever shall be,
when Jesus knew that he was going to the cross,
he promised his disciples
that they would not be left alone.
Jesus assured them that the Holy Spirit
would remain with them,
teaching them how to live,
and reminding them of all he had said.
Weeks later, when the day of Pentecost arrived,
you poured out your Spirit,
giving your disciples the power to speak
in many languages,
and making tongues of flame
dance above their heads.
Today, we ask that you pour out your Spirit on us,
giving us the wisdom and the courage
to live in peace as Jesus's followers. Amen.

Proclamation and Response

Prayer of Confession (Acts 2, John 14)

Spirit of truth, Giver of visions, Sender of dreams,
our hearts remain troubled and afraid.
For we fear the future,
forgetting your promise
to do whatever we ask in your name.
You promise to fill us with new vision,
to give us gifts of prophecy and dreams.
Yet, we act as if we are on our own,
forgetting your promise
to fill us with your Spirit.
You tell us that we are not alone,
that you are always with us.
Forgive us when we forget,
and we fail to keep your commandments
to love you and one another.

Words of Assurance (John 14)

Hear the good news: the Holy Spirit is always with us,
filling us with prophecy, visions, and dreams.
In the name of Jesus Christ, you are forgiven.
In the name of Jesus Christ, you are forgiven.
Glory to God. Amen.

Passing the Peace of Christ (Romans 8)

We did not receive a spirit of slavery to fall back into
fear, but have received a spirit of adoption into Christ's
body of love. In this hope and promise, let us share signs
of peace with one another.
The peace of Christ be with you.
The peace of Christ be with you always.

Response to the Word (Acts 2, Romans 8, John 14)

Giver of visions, Sender of dreams, Spirit of truth,
    you fill us with new vision
    and offer us new dreams.
In the hearing of your word,
    our hearts are no longer troubled or afraid.
    Amen.

Thanksgiving and Communion

Offering Prayer (Acts 2)

Sender of dreams, Spirit of truth, Giver of visions,
    accept these gifts and offerings,
        as evidence of the holy fire
            burning in our hearts. Amen.

Great Thanksgiving

Christ be with you.
    And also with you.
Lift up your hearts.
    We lift them up to God.
Let us give our thanks to the Holy One.
    It is right to give our thanks and praise.

It is a right, good, and a joyful thing
    always and everywhere to give our thanks to you,
    who poured out tongues of fire on the disciples
    at Pentecost.
You promised to give our young people
    visions of a better world,
    and our elders dreams of peace.
All who are led by your Spirit are your children,
    joint heirs with Christ in both suffering and glory.

And so, with your creatures on earth
    and all the heavenly chorus,
    we praise your name and join their unending hymn:
    Holy, holy, holy Lord, God of power and might,
        heaven and earth are full of your glory.
    Hosanna in the highest. Blessed is the one
        who comes in the name of the Lord.
    Hosanna in the highest.

Holy are you, and holy is your child, Jesus,
    who sent the Holy Spirit to be with us,
    so that we would not be left alone.

On the night in which he gave himself up,
    Jesus took bread, broke it, saying,
    "Take, eat, all of you.
    This is my body, broken for you.
    Whenever you eat it,
    do so in remembrance of me."
After supper, he took the cup, saying,
    "This is the cup of the new covenant,
    poured out for the healing of the world.
    Whenever you drink it,
    do so in remembrance of me."

And so, in remembrance of your mighty acts
    in Jesus Christ, we proclaim the mystery of faith.
    Christ has died.
    Christ is risen.
    Christ will come again.
Pour out your Holy Spirit on us,
    and on these gifts of grain and grape,
        fruit of the earth and work of human hands.

Make them be for us the body and blood of Christ,
that we may be the body of Christ,
filled with the fire of the Holy Spirit
for the healing of the world.
Sender of dreams, Spirit of truth, giver of visions,
you are the one God to whom we offer our praise
and thanks.
Amen.

Sending Forth

Benediction (John 14:27 NRSV)

Jesus said, "Peace I leave with you;
my peace I give to you.
Do not let your hearts be troubled,
and do not let them be afraid."
With hearts afire and filled with new visions,
let us go in peace to love and serve the world.
Amen.

June 12, 2022

Trinity Sunday
Jamie D. Greening

Color

White

Scripture Readings

Proverbs 8:1-4, 22-31, Psalm 8, Romans 5:1-5,
John 16:12-15

Theme Ideas

In Proverbs, Wisdom calls out like a wise woman, warning and encouraging us at the crossroads of life. In
Psalm 8, the call is about the nature of creation, while in
Romans 5, the Lord calls out to us about faith, grace, and
salvation in Christ. In John 16, the Holy Spirit beckons
us into the path of truth. Wisdom is spiritual enlighten-
ment, and in each of these readings, we find that she is
calling us to a deeper understanding of and relationship
with God.

Invitation and Gathering

Centering Words (Proverbs 8)

Wisdom is calling. She calls from the highest heavens and speaks with truth on her lips, calling all people to faith, peace, hope, and love.

Call to Worship (Proverbs 8, Romans 5, John 16)

To you, O people, wisdom calls.
She calls out to each of us:
>   beckoning us to experience peace in Christ,
>   harkening us to discover the truth of life;
>   imploring us to know true love,
>   as it is poured into our heart.
Wisdom calls.
Let us answer her call,
>   as we celebrate faith in the one
>   who leads us into life.

–Or–

Call to Worship (Psalm 8)

(The attributes of God are said by eight different people, scattered throughout the worship space.)
O Lord, our Sovereign, you are:
>   *Majestic,*
>   *Compassionate,*
>   *Glorious,*
>   *Inspiring,*
>   *Beautiful,*
>   *Amazing,*
>   *Tender,*
>   *Powerful.*
Your name is blessed in all the earth.

Opening Prayer (Proverbs 8, Psalm 8)

O Lord, you reveal wisdom and spiritual insight
    through your presence in creation.
When we look at the heavens,
    we see your vastness.
When we look at seas teeming with fish
    and verdant fields painted like a canvas,
        we see your creativity and your bounty.
For all of this and for so much more,
    we praise your name. Amen.

–Or–

Opening Prayer (Romans 5, John 16)

We thank you, O Lord,
    for giving us love and peace,
        through your Son, Christ Jesus;
        for offering us the key to all spiritual knowledge,
        through your Holy Spirit.
To those who are in the midst of life's problems,
    grant your wisdom and insight from above.
To those who are burdened with anxiety and fear,
    offer your wise assurance in times of need.
To those facing decisions about family or career,
    bless them with your wisdom on high.
To those entering a new chapter in their lives—
    be it the birth of children, taking a new jobs,
    finding a place to live, or entering retirement—
        guide them on the proper path,
        and bless them with a sense of peace.
This we pray in the name and wisdom
    of Jesus Christ, our Lord. Amen.

Proclamation and Response

Prayer of Confession (Proverbs 8, Psalm 8, Romans 5, John 16)

God of infinite mercy, be with us in our need.
When we neglect the wisdom
of knowing our place in this world,
forgive us.
When we trade your peace and calls for unity
for conflict and violence,
heal us.
When we forsake good character
to join those who scoff at your ways,
restore us.
When we ignore your truth,
and turn our back on your wisdom,
ennoble and enlighten us.
Forgive us and renew us, Lord,
that we may abide in your truth
and live in your love forever. Amen.

Words of Assurance (Romans 5)

Through the power of the Holy Spirit,
God fills our souls with grace and wisdom.
It is from this grace that we have hope.
It is from this wisdom that we know God's love.
It is from the living God
that we find life and forgiveness.

Passing the Peace (Romans 5)

Since we have peace with God through Jesus Christ, let
us turn and share this peace with one another.

Introduction to the Word (Proverbs 8, Psalm 8, Romans 5)

I hear a noise. I hear a sound. Do you hear it?
>**It is wisdom calling.**

Where is she? Where can I find her?
>**She calls from the highest heavens,**
>**and speaks with truth on her lips.**

May I come? May I learn?
>**Yes, you may come. You may learn.**
>**Wisdom calls all people**
>**to faith, peace, hope, and love.**

Response to the Words (Proverbs 8, Psalm 8, Romans 5, John 16)

Teach us your wisdom, O Lord,
>that we may live wisely, not foolishly.

Open our minds to understand our place in the world,
>that we may be proper stewards and caretakers
>>of this beautiful earth.

May your love and wisdom flow through us
>into this world of hatred and mistrust,
>>that we may sow the seeds of peace.

Illumine our hearts to the path of truth, Holy Spirit,
>that we may celebrate the ways that lead to life.

Amen.

Thanksgiving And Commmunion

Invitation to the Offering (Proverbs 8, Psalm 8)

Through holy wisdom, the Lord has made the world as a rich dwelling place, giving us stewardship over the created order. As God is mindful of us and of our needs, let us now be mindful of our obligation to the needs of others, through our generosity and responsibility for God's gifts.

Offering Prayer (Proverbs 8, Psalm 8)

O Lord, we rejoice with thankful hearts,
> that you have given us this beautiful world
>> in which to work and play—
>>> a world full of your wisdom and majesty.

We offer praise with deepest gratitude
> for blessing us with your bounty.

As we return a portion of your blessings to you,
> use these offerings, these tokens of our devotion
>> to increase wisdom in the world,
>> protect the created order,
>> bless the vulnerable,
>> heal the sick,
>>> and comfort the afflicted. Amen.

Invitation to Communion (Proverbs 8, Psalm 8, Romans 5, John 16)

(Consider using as a call and response between two readers)
Wisdom calls:
> **Come eat the bread of life.**

Wisdom calls:
> **Come drink the cup of fellowship.**

Wisdom calls:
> **Come partake of truth and grace.**

Wisdom calls:
> **Come and be enlightened by the Holy Spirit.**

Communion Prayer (Proverbs 8, Psalm 8, Romans 5, John 16)

Almighty, majestic, and sovereign Lord,
>our hearts are stirred by the power of your wisdom.

In the very elements of creation,
>you display your power and might
>>for every soul to perceive.

And yet, a deeper wisdom is revealed
>in the bread and the cup.

As we partake of these simple yet profound elements,
>whisper into our hearts,
>>and speak the truth we long to hear.

Holy Spirit, guide us into truth about ourselves,
>our world, our church, and your ways,
>>that we may be transformed.

Open our eyes to deep spiritual wisdom,
>as we participate in the ancient work
>>of Holy Communion.

Sending Forth

Benediction (Proverbs 8, Romans 5)

Through grace and peace,
we have wisdom we need to be transformed.
>**For sufferings leads to endurance,**
>**endurance gives rise to character,**
>**and character produces hope.**

In the true hope founded in God,
we are never disappointed.

June 19, 2022

Second Sunday after Pentecost
Proper 7
Father's Day
Mary Petrina Boyd

Color

Green

Scripture Readings

1 Kings 19:1-4 (5-7) 8-15a; Psalm 42; Galatians 3:23-29;
Luke 8:26-39

Theme Ideas

We hunger for God's presence. The psalm expresses a
deep longing for God. Discouraged, Elijah is renewed
by God's presence in the wilderness. The man whom
Jesus healed longed to be free of what possessed him.
And finally, we are all gathered together as the family
of God. No one is left behind. God is present with us all.

Invitation and Gathering

Centering Words (Psalm 42, Galatians 3)

We hunger for the holy, longing for the living God. We gather as children of God, rejoicing in the promise.

Call to Worship (1 Kings 19, Galatians 3)

We come as children of God.
We come, unsure where to seek
God's presence.
The wind blows,
but God is not in the wind.
The earth quakes,
but God is not in the earthquake.
The fire burns,
but God is not in the flame.
There is nothing but utter stillness.
God is there in the silence.
In silence we will wait for God.
God is with us now.
(Remain in silence for a few moments before moving to the next element of worship.)

–Or–

Call to Worship (Galatians 3)

We come as children of God.
Everyone is welcome here.
Everyone?
Yes everyone!
What about those who are different from us?
They are part of God's family.
Then we are really all one?
We are one in Christ Jesus.

Opening Prayer or Prayer of Yearning (Psalm 42)

Come, O God, be with us here.
As much as a deer longs for streams of cool water,
> we long to know that you are with us.
When trouble and sorrow come,
> we need you.
Help us remember that you are always with us,
> and that your love is steadfast.
Put your song into our hearts,
> that we may praise you this day. Amen.

Proclamation and Response

Prayer of Confession (1 Kings, Psalm 42, Galatians 3, Luke 8)

We long for you, O God,
> discouraged by our flagging efforts.
We are afraid of what the future may bring.
We separate ourselves from our siblings in Christ
> because they are different from us.
When we pray,
> we don't always feel that you hear us.
Be present with us.
Heal the places of our doubt, despair,
> and alienation.
Cure us from hatred and discrimination.
Cast out all that keeps us from you
> and from one another. Amen.

Words of Assurance (Psalm 42, Galatians 3)

Each day, God's love is steadfast.
Each night, God's peace abides with us.
We are all part of one family in Christ Jesus.

Passing the Peace of Christ (Galatians 3)

There is no longer Jew or Greek; there is no longer slave or free; there is no longer male or female, for all are one in Christ Jesus. Share this gracious welcome with one another.

Response to the Word (Galatians 3)

God of all, enlarge our hearts,
    that we may recognize each person
        as part of your beloved family.
Tear down the walls of prejudice and racism
    that divide us.
Grant us the vision to look at the stranger
    and see your face.
Remind us that the things that divide us—
    gender, race, economic and social status,
    religion, and education—
        are not important in your eyes.
For we are all one in Christ Jesus. Amen.

Thanksgiving and Communion

Offering Prayer (Galatians 3)

Generous God, you are always with us,
    always caring for us,
        always drawing us together.
We are so grateful for your loving presence.
We bring our gifts before you today,
    that this offering may reach out in love
        to your people everywhere. Amen.

Sending Forth

Benediction (Luke 8:39 NRSV)

Jesus told the one who was healed and whole:
>"Return to your home,
>and declare how much God has done for you."

As our service ends, we too return to our homes.
In all that we do and say,
>let us declare how much God has done for us.

June 26, 2022

Third Sunday after Pentecost
Proper 8
Mary Scifres

Copyright © Mary Scifres

Color

Green

Scripture Readings

2 Kings 2:1-2, 6-14; Psalm 77:1-2, 11-20;
Galatians 5:1, 13-25; Luke 9:51-62

Theme Ideas

Even as the Ordinary Season begins, with each lection standing on its own, a common theme emerges in today's scripture readings: the power of being led by God's Spirit in relationship with others who are also led by God's Spirit. Together, Elijah and Elisha travel to Elijah's ascension, with a company of prophets standing nearby. Likewise, Jesus prepares for his journey to Jerusalem with his close disciples, James and John, even as he invites others onto the journey with them. Even the Galatians are invited as a community, rather than just as individuals, to live by the Spirit and to enjoy the freedom of life in the Spirit. Such is the journey of following God's Spirit—a journey best traveled with companions alongside, a journey that intermingles freedom and obligation.

Invitation and Gathering

Centering Words or Opening Prayer (Galatians 5)

Lead us, Holy Spirit.

Guide us in the power of your ways,
> that we may grow in love, joy, peace, patience,
>> kindness, generosity, faithfulness, gentleness,
>> and self-control.

Call to Worship (Galatians 5)

The Spirit is here,
> **inviting us to worship.**

The Spirit is here,
> **in each of our lives.**

The Spirit is here,
> **in our gathered community.**

The Spirit is here,
> **guiding us together in love, peace,**
> **and patience.**

Opening Prayer (Galatians 5)

Speak to us, Spirit of wisdom and truth,
> as we worship this day.

Bind us together into a community of love and peace.

Live and move in our lives,
that we may grow in your Spirit,
deepen our faithfulness,
and display the love, peace, patience,
kindness, and generosity
you have planted in our souls.

Proclamation and Response

Prayer of Yearning (Galatians 5)
Spirit of love, you know the yearning for love
that rests in each and every one of us.
Help us love one another,
even when hatred and anger well within us.
Bring us peace and patience,
even when restlessness and enmity fill our hearts.
Inspire us to live with generosity of spirit
when we are immersed in self-centered thoughts
and selfish actions.
Shower us with joy and hope
when fear and despair are all around.
Bear your fruit in our lives,
through the power of your grace and forgiveness,
that we may be children of your Spirit,
living by your power
and following where you lead.
In gratitude and trust, we pray. Amen.

Words of Assurance (Galatians 5)
If we live by the Spirit, we will be guided by the Spirit.
Guided by the Spirit, we are children of the Spirit,
healed by God's love, and blessed by Christ's grace.

Passing the Peace of Christ (Galatians 5)
> As children of the Spirit, let us be a community of peace,
> sharing signs of kindness and love with one another.

Introduction to the Word (Psalm 77, Galatians 5)
> Call to mind the deeds of God,
> > as you listen for the Spirit this day.
>
> Meditate on God's work,
> > and muse on the message that Spirit seeks to share.

Response to the Word (Galatians 5)
> In freedom, we are called to live the law of love.
> > **In freedom, we are given the Spirit.**
>
> For it is the Spirit that leads us to grow:
> > **in love, joy, peace and patience;**
>
> in kindness, generosity, and faithfulness;
> > **in gentleness and self-control.**
>
> It is the Spirit who invites us to nourish God's world,
> > **with these gifts that are growing within us.**

Thanksgiving and Communion

Offering Prayer (2 Kings 2, Galatians 5)
> Bear fruit with these gifts we now bring, Holy One.
> May they bring a double share of your presence
> > to all who are touched by them.
>
> Bless us also, who have given so generously,
> > that we may grow in your Spirit,
> > > bringing even more generosity and love
> > > > to your world. Amen.

Sending Forth

Benediction (Galatians 5)

Go to be fruitful in all that you do!
Bring love, joy, peace, and patience
    to everyone you meet.
Share kindness, gentleness, and generosity
    in every encounter.
In doing so, you not only live by the Spirit,
    you bring the Spirit with you.

July 3, 2022

Fourth Sunday after Pentecost
Proper 9
B. J. Beu

Color

Green

Scripture Readings

2 Kings 5:1-14; Psalm 30; Galatians 6:(1-6) 7-16;
Luke 10:1-11, 16-20

Theme Ideas

God is there to save us, but works in mysterious ways. In
2 Kings, a Hebrew captive entreats her master, Naaman,
to travel to Israel so that he might be healed of leprosy.
Another foreign servant convinces Naaman to do as the
prophet Elisha bids, that Naaman may indeed be made
clean. In Luke's Gospel, Jesus sends seventy followers
out to share God's blessings and peace, knowing he is
sending them out, "like lambs into the midst of wolves"
(10:3 NRSV). Galatians urges us to correct transgressors

in a spirit of gentleness. True power, godly power, seems to come from those who have every reason to withhold it.

Invitation and Gathering

Centering Words (Galatians 6, Luke 10)

God works through us when we are generous of spirit and the gentle of heart. Though we may feel like lambs in the midst of wolves, our ministries can change the world.

Call to Worship (Psalm 30)

Weeping may linger for the night,
but joy comes with the morning.
Sing praises to our God.
Give thanks to the Lord of hosts.
God's anger may flash for a moment,
but God's favor lasts a lifetime.
Sing praises to the Lord.
Worship the God of our salvation.

Opening Prayer (2 Kings 5, Psalm 30, Galatians 6, Luke 10:9)

God of unexpected mercies and fierce challenges,
　　it can be disorienting to be your people.
You turn our mourning into dancing,
　　then you send us forth like lambs
　　　　into the midst of wolves.
You turn our weeping into shouts of joy,
　　then you charge us to seek the welfare of those
　　　　who have abused and betrayed us.
You turn our scarcity into overflowing abundance,
　　then you instruct us to leave it all behind
　　　　and seek those who have gone astray.

Help us question our deeply held assumptions
and challenge our unconscious convictions.
Grant us the courage to speak Christ's word of peace
and to share Christ's word of comfort:
"The kingdom of God has come near." Amen.

Proclamation and Response

Prayer of Confession (2 Kings 5, Galatians 6, Luke 10)

Merciful God, you reveal yourself in mysterious ways.
Those we have been taught to admire
have proven untrustworthy,
while those we have been taught to mistrust
have proven to be vehicles of your love
and your grace.
Those we have looked to for wisdom
have proven to be false prophets,
while those we have dismissed out of hand
have been avenues of your truth.
Wash us clean of our arrogance and presumption,
and heal us of deeply held prejudices.
Open our hearts to all who have generous spirits
humble hearts, and gentle natures,
whoever they may be.
And open our ears to the many ways
you are speaking still. Amen.

Words of Assurance (Psalm 30, Luke 10)

God's anger may last a moment,
but God's favor lasts a lifetime.

Weeping may last the night,
>
> but joy comes in the morning.

Rejoice and be glad,
>
> for our names are written in heaven.

Passing the Peace of Christ (Luke 10)

Sisters and brothers in Christ, we are like lambs in the midst of wolves. Still, Christ calls us to share blessings of peace. Turn to one another and share signs of this peace, that we may draw strength for the work Christ calls us to do.

Response to the Word (Galatians 6, Luke 10)

Are you generous of spirit and gentle of heart?
Are you ready to be sent out as lambs
>
> into the midst of wolves?

Don't despair.
God has equipped you for the tasks ahead.
With gentleness and words of peace,
>
> look to the welfare of all.

Thanksgiving and Communion

Invitation to the Offering (Psalm 30)

Weeping may last the night, but joy comes with the morning. God has turned our tears into shouts of thanksgiving. Let us be grateful for the many blessings in our lives, as we collect today's offering.

Offering Prayer (Luke 10)

Bountiful God, the harvest is plentiful,
>
> but the laborers are few.

May the offerings we bring before you this day
be a sign of our commitment
to labor in your vineyard.
May the gifts we share with the world
reflect our commitment
to bring your kingdom here on earth,
as it is in heaven. Amen.

Sending Forth

Benediction (Galatians 6, Luke 10)

In the spirit of Christ,
bear one another's burdens;
correct one another with gentleness;
and heal one another with signs of peace.
Rejoice as you leave this place,
for if you persevere in doing what is right,
you will reap a harvest of joy, hope, and love.
Go with the peace of God.

July 10, 2022

Fifth Sunday after Pentecost
Proper 10
B. J. Beu

Color

Green

Scripture Readings

Amos 7:7-17; Psalm 82; Colossians 1:1-14;
Luke 10:25-37

Theme Ideas

Divine and human judgment focus these readings. In
Amos, God uses a plumb line to judge Israel, finding
it wanting. The psalmist calls God to take up the roll of
judge once again, wondering how long the sins of the
wicked and the powerful will be tolerated to the detri-
ment of the weak and the orphan. Having heard of the
faith of the Colossians, Paul judges them worthy of their
calling. Faithfulness leads to growth in grace, love, truth,
and life. Asked by a lawyer, "Who is my neighbor?" Jesus tells the well-known parable of the Good Samaritan,

and asks the man to judge for himself who his neighbor is. Although we often react negatively to the idea of judging, these passages make clear that sound judgment can be a righteous enterprise. We are called to righteous judgment, without becoming judgmental.

Invitation and Gathering

Centering Words (Amos 7, Colossians 1, Luke 10)

God sets a plumb line to judge how we care for our neighbor. Jesus tells the parable of the Good Samaritan to teach us how to be a good neighbor. Everything hangs in the balance.

Call to Worship (Luke 10)

Love the Lord your God with all your heart,
with all your soul, with all your strength,
and with all of your mind.
> **We will worship God, the one we love.**
Love your neighbor as yourself.
> **We will open our hearts to all God's children.**

–Or–

Call to Worship (Psalm 82)

Shout to the Lord, you people of God.
Bring your petitions before the judgment seat.
> **Worship the one who hears our cries,**
> **rescues the perishing, and lifts up the lowly.**
Call to the Lord, you disciples of Christ.
Proclaim your case before God's holy council.

Worship the one who heeds our pleas,
frees the captives, and sustains the widows
and the orphans.
Sing to the Lord, you children of the Most High.
Declare your need before our righteous judge.
Worship the one who responds to our needs,
heals our wounds, and fills our world with light.

Opening Prayer (Colossians 1, Luke 10)

God of power and might, turn our hearts of stone
into hearts of flesh.
For only in loving can we lead lives
worthy of your calling.
Grant us the courage to live with the saints
in the glory of your love.
And fill us with your grace and peace,
that we may know the richness
of eternal life in your Spirit,
through Jesus Christ, our Lord. Amen.

Proclamation and Response

Prayer of Yearning (Amos 7, Psalm 82, Colossians 1, Luke 10)

Judge us in your righteousness, Holy One,
and show us who we truly are,
for we long to see ourselves as you see us.
Against the plumb line of your justice,
our ways seem out of balance,
and our practices seem wanting.

We yearn for the day when the powerful
　　will no longer deny justice
　　　　to the weak and destitute,
　　　　　　or turn a blind eye to the wicked.
We long for the time when those who live at ease
　　will no longer ignore the plight of the poor,
　　　　or turn away from those living paycheck
　　　　　　to paycheck.
Show us what it means to be a good neighbor,
　　that our works may bear good fruit,
　　　　and that our lives may shine the light
　　　　　　of your justice. Amen.

Words of Assurance (Luke 10)

Eternal life is ours when we love the Lord our God
　　with all our heart, with all our soul,
　　with all our strength, and with all our mind;
　　and when we love our neighbor as ourselves.

Passing the Peace of Christ (Colossians 1)

Love of God and neighbor is the path to eternal life. Rejoicing in the love that flows within, when we abide in Christ's peace, share this peace with your neighbor.

Response to the Word Or Benediction (Colossians 1, Luke 10)

Let us be people who bear the fruit of eternal life:
　　loving God with all our heart,
　　with all of our soul,
　　with all of our strength,
　　and with all of our mind;
　　and loving our neighbor as ourselves.
Love well and you will live.

Thanksgiving and Communion

Offering Prayer (Psalm 82, Colossians 1, Luke 10)

Bountiful God,
> your love bears the fruit of hope and grace;
> your ways lead to fullness of life.

May today's offering bear fruit in our world,
> that your love may cause old hatreds to cease,
> > old wounds heal, and old divisions mend.

Amen.

Sending Forth

Benediction (Psalm 82, Colossians 1, Luke 10)

Go forth in the strength of God's glorious power.
Go forth in the hope and peace of Christ.
Go forth in the power of the Holy Spirit.
Go with God.

July 17, 2022

Sixth Sunday after Pentecost
Proper 11

Joanne Carlson Brown

Color

Green

Scripture Readings

Amos 8:1-12, Psalm 52, Colossians 1:15-28, Luke 10: 38-42

Theme Ideas

At first glance, these scriptures are tied together because God is not pleased with the people: neglecting the poor, greedy attitudes, dishonesty, and being hospitable, but not in the way we are to be. It doesn't feel very uplifting for a Sunday in July. But maybe people do need to "sweat it out"—recognizing how we too often please ourselves, feel self-righteous, and try to do what the world says is right. But in the midst of God's displeasure, God's love remains—offering forgiveness and right relationship. Still, we need to change our ways to walk in the way of God.

Invitation and Gathering

Centering Words (Colossians 1)

Even when we forget that God watches over us, God loves and redeems us.

Call to Worship (Amos 8, Psalm 52, Luke 10)

Come from the busyness and the business of the day.
We come to let go of the ways of the world.
Come and turn aside the temptation to do the things that are only done in the shadows.
We come to embrace what God offers us,
God's presence and unconditional love.
Come, however hesitantly, to find refuge
and the way to live in Christ's great love.

Opening Prayer (Amos 8, Psalm 52, Colossians 1, Luke 10)

As we come before you God,
in the presence of our sisters and brothers,
help us look honestly at our lives
and see what you want them to be.
Help us perceive the things and attitudes
we need to change.
As we open ourselves to your healing presence,
fill us with the Spirit of your love and wholeness.
Amen.

Proclamation and Response

Prayer of Confession (Amos 8, Psalm 52, Luke 10)

The world seems to be going to hell in a handbasket.
Much as we don't intend to,

we seem to jump into that basket
  instead of into your loving arms.
Many of the world's values
  have infiltrated our minds, and hearts,
    and actions.
It happens so gradually, we hardly notice.
We place value on things that harm us,
  and we insist that things be
    the way we think they should be.
We lost our way,
  but we are here now.
We want to be people who walk in your way,
  not those who wander blindly from the path.
We lay ourselves before you,
  trusting in your steadfast love. Amen.

Words of Assurance (Colossians 1)

There is nothing we can do
  that will make God love us any less.
We can disappoint God.
We can ignore God's way.
But God is always there on the way—
  guiding us, calling us to live
  in God's unconditional, steadfast love.
Open yourselves to this love,
  knowing that with God,
  all things can be made right.

Passing the Peace (Psalm 52)

Greet one another as sisters and brothers walking the way of God.

Prayer of Preparation (Luke 10)

God, you show us your way
in the words of scripture.
May we hear and speak your word,
through these readings
and the teachings they share.
May we, like Mary, sit at your feet and listen.

Response to the Word (Luke 10)

Having sat at your feet and listened,
help us put what we have heard into practice.

Thanksgiving and Communion

Invitation to the Offering (Amos 8, Psalm 52, Luke 10)

We heard today of people who did not offer the things
they ought to, especially to the most vulnerable among
us. Sometimes we offer what we think is best, only to realize that it isn't what you want us to give. May we offer
you now our very selves: our energy, our resources, and
our time. Help us reach the vulnerable; and enable this
church to be a place of refuge, help, justice, love, and
hospitality.

Offering Prayer (Amos 8, Psalm 52, Luke 10)

Most loving God, most welcoming God,
we bring these gifts to you,
knowing that you will use them
according to your purposes.
We dedicate ourselves to your way,
to challenge the worldly values
that are so prevalent in your world today. Amen.

Sending Forth

Benediction

In a world that tries to impose its values on us,
   live the way of God.
Challenge injustice, aid those in need, listen intently,
   and do not be preoccupied with busyness.
Share what you have heard, so that, together,
   we may transform the world
   into the beloved community of God.
Go with the strength God gives us,
   the love God gives us through Jesus,
   and the fire the Holy Spirit offers
   to keep us going no matter what. Amen.

July 24, 2022

Seventh Sunday after Pentecost
Proper 12
Deborah Sokolove

Color

Green

Scripture Readings

Hosea 1:2-10; Psalm 85; Colossians 2:6-15 (16-19);
Luke 11:1-13

Theme Ideas

Although it can seem that God has turned away from us,
or that we are being rejected for our failings, the truth is
much different: God's love is always with us. No matter
what we have done or how long we have turned away,
we are always beloved children of the living God. Like
a good parent, God gives us the bread of life, so that we
have what we need to feed the world with love.

Invitation and Gathering

Centering Words (Luke 11)

If we, who are merely human, give our children the food
they need, how much more will the Holy Spirit give to
those who are beloved by God?

Call to Worship (Psalm 85)

We gather to hear what the Holy One will speak.
God will speak peace to the faithful,
those who turn to love in their hearts.
Surely wholeness is at hand for those who stand in awe.
Show us your steadfast love, Holy One,
and grant us your wholeness and peace.
Let steadfast love and faithfulness meet us today.
Let us worship the God who calls us.

Opening Prayer (Hosea 1, Psalm 85, Luke 11)

Holy Mystery, in ancient days,
    you spoke to your prophet Hosea,
        telling him to give his children names
            that warned of hard times to come.
Even though the people heard,
    "You are not my people,"
        you insisted that they remained
        your beloved children.
When his disciples asked him how to pray,
    Jesus called them beloved children of God,
        telling them to ask only for each day's bread.
Today, we stand in awe, waiting to hear your word,
    yearning to know that we, too,
        are your beloved children.

Give us the bread that we need today,
>   so that we might feed a world
>   that hungers for wholeness. Amen.

Proclamation and Response

Prayer of Confession (Luke 11:2-4 NRSV)

Jesus said, when you pray, say,
>   "Give us each day our daily bread."
>   **Yet we hoard our money, our time, and our love,**
>   **wanting much more than what we need each day.**
Jesus said, say to your Father and Mother in heaven,
>   "Forgive us our sins, for we ourselves forgive everyone
>   indebted to us."
>   **Still, we hold grudges, refusing to forgive,**
>   **even when the debt is paid.**
Jesus said, say to the Holy One,
>   "Hallowed be your name. Your kingdom come."
>   **Holy Mystery, forgive the times**
>   **we take your name in vain,**
>   **and heal our refusal to live each day**
>   **in your holy realm.**

Words of Assurance (Luke 11)

Hear the good news:
>   If you, who are merely human,
>   know how to give good gifts to your children,
>   how much more will the Holy Spirit
>   come to those who ask?
In the name of Jesus Christ, you are forgiven.
>   **In the name of Jesus Christ, you are forgiven.**
>   **Glory to God. Amen.**

Passing the Peace of Christ (Luke 11)

As forgiven and loved children of God, as those who are filled with the Holy Spirit, let us share signs of peace with one another.
The peace of Christ be with you.
The peace of Christ be with you always.

Response to the Word (Luke 11)

Holy giver of good gifts, we give you thanks
for feeding us with your word,
and for filling us with your Spirit.
Use us to bring your gifts to a hungry world. Amen.

Thanksgiving and Communion

Offering Prayer (Luke 11)

Generous Giver, having received so much from you,
we offer our tithes and offerings into your hands,
that they may bring hope and gladness
to a hurting world. Amen.

Great Thanksgiving

Christ be with you.
And also with you.
Lift up your hearts.
We lift them up to God.
Let us give our thanks to the Holy One.
It is right to give our thanks and praise.

It is a right, good, and a joyful thing,
always and everywhere, to give our thanks to you,
who give what is good to all your beloved children,
showing your steadfast love throughout the ages.

Righteousness goes before you,
    making a path for your steps.
You speak peace to your people, to your faithful,
    and to all who turn to you in their hearts.

And so, with your creatures on earth
    and all the heavenly chorus,
    we praise your name and join their unending hymn:
    Holy, holy, holy Lord, God of power and might,
        heaven and earth are full of your glory.
    Hosanna in the highest. Blessed is the one
        who comes in the name of the Lord.
    Hosanna in the highest.

Holy are you, and holy is your child, Jesus,
    who taught us to pray,
    promising that everyone who asks receives,
    and everyone who searches finds.
For, everyone who knocks, the door will be opened.

On the night in which he gave himself up,
    Jesus took bread, broke it, saying,
    "Take, eat, all of you.
    This is my body, broken for you.
    Whenever you eat it,
    do so in remembrance of me."
After supper, he took the cup, saying,
    "This is the cup of the new covenant,
    poured out for the healing of the world.
    Whenever you drink it,
    do so in remembrance of me."

And so, in remembrance of your mighty acts
    in Jesus Christ, we proclaim the mystery of faith.

Christ has died.
Christ is risen.
Christ will come again.

Pour out your Holy Spirit on us,
and on these gifts of grain and grape,
fruit of the earth and work of human hands.
Make them be for us the body and blood of Christ,
that we may be the body of Christ,
feeding a world that hungers for wholeness.

Holy Mystery, Holy Word, Holy Breath,
you are the one God to whom we offer our praise
and thanks.
Amen.

Sending Forth

Benediction (Colossians 2, Luke 11)
As you have received Christ Jesus,
continue to live your lives in him.
Remain rooted and built up in him,
abounding in thanksgiving
and established in true faith,
just as you were taught.
Forgiven, loved, and filled with the Holy Spirit,
let us go in peace to love and serve the world.
Amen.

July 31, 2022

Eighth Sunday after Pentecost
Proper 13

B. J. Beu

Copyright © B. J. Beu

Color

Green

Scripture Readings

Hosea 11:1-11; Psalm 107:1-9, 43; Colossians 3:1-11;
Luke 12:13-21

Theme Ideas

Today's scriptures portray God's faithfulness, even in
the face of radical disobedience and unrighteous behavior. In Hosea, God laments that Israel and Ephraim,
whom God suckled like a nursing mother, has turned
to serve other gods. Yet God's wrath is stilled, and hope
is offered, that the people may return from exile. The
psalmist praises God's steadfast goodness. Colossians
warns us that our true lives are hidden with Christ in
God, and we should avoid reveling in earthly pleasures
and unrighteous behavior. Treat everyone with equal

respect, for we are one in Christ Jesus. In Luke, Jesus warns against the powers of greed, teaching us to store up treasures for ourselves in heaven, not on earth.

Invitation and Gathering

Centering Words (Luke 12)

To be secure in earthly treasure, but not rich toward God, is to be poor indeed.

Call to Worship (Psalm 107)

Give thanks to the Lord,
for God is good.
> **God's steadfast love endures forever.**

Make your petitions heard,
for God saves us in times of trouble.
> **Christ's steadfast love endures forever.**

God satisfies our hunger with good things,
and quenches our thirst with living water.
> **The Spirit's steadfast love endures forever.**

Let us worship.

–Or–

Call to Worship (Psalm 107)

Sing praises to our God.
> **God's love is sure.**
> **Christ's love never ends.**

Shout for joy, all the earth.
> **God's grace satisfies the thirsty.**
> **The Spirit fills the hungry with good things.**

Proclaim the Lord's glory.
> **God's salvation is sure.**
> **God's faithfulness never ends.**

Opening Prayer (Colossians 3)

Eternal God, as people raised with Christ,
　　teach us to seek the things that are above,
　　　　where Christ abides in glory.
Even as our true lives remain hidden in you with Christ,
　　grant us a glimpse of our true selves,
　　　　made pure and whole in your love.
Renew your Spirit within us,
　　and make us fit to bear the glory of your image.
Amen.

Proclamation and Response

Prayer of Yearning (Colossians 3, Luke 12)

Loving God, you show us the blessedness
　　of seeking things that are above,
　　　　but our hearts are captured by the shiny objects
　　　　　　that catch our eye and capture our attention.
When we lose sight of our priorities,
　　heal our desire to get our share.
Help us store up treasure in heaven
　　rather than here on earth.
Renew us in your Spirit this day,
　　that our lives, hidden with Christ,
　　　　may be revealed with Christ in glory. Amen.

Words of Assurance (Colossians 3)

We, who have been raised with Christ,
　　are heirs of his glory.
When we store up treasures in heaven,
　　we are rich in God's blessings,
　　　　and sealed in the embrace of God's love.

Passing the Peace of Christ (Luke 12)

The peace of Christ is knowing how to store treasures in heaven. Let us share this peace with one another, that we may be rich in God's love, each and every day of our lives.

Response to the Word (Colossians 3, Luke 12)

Set your minds on things that are above,
that you may be raised to new life in Christ.
Then, when Christ, who is our life, is revealed,
we will be revealed with him in glory.
Until then, our lives are hidden in God with Christ.
And that is good news.

–Or–

Response to the Word (Psalm 107, Colossians 3)

God has fed us with the words of holy scripture.
Fed by God's word,
our hunger is satisfied.
Christ has quenched our thirst with living water.
Nourished by God's Spirit,
our thirst is quenched.
The Spirit has hidden us in God with Christ.
Renewed in the Spirit,
we wait to be revealed with Christ in glory.

Thanksgiving and Communion

Offering Prayer (Psalm 107)

We sing your praises, O God,
for your love is sure and true,
your faithfulness is never ending.
You satisfy the thirsty
and fill the hungry with good things.

Receive the offerings we bring before you this day,
that these gifts may continue your work
of tending the needy,
providing hope for the downtrodden,
and blessing those who live in want.
In Christ's name, we pray. Amen.

Sending Forth

Benediction (Colossians 3)

Go forth as people who have been raised
with Christ to newness of life.
We go as Christ's disciples.
Go forth as people whose lives are hidden with Christ
in the living God.
We go to bear the mystery of life with Christ.
Go forth as people who will be revealed in glory
when Christ's glory is revealed.
We go to store up treasure in heaven,
where Christ is seated at the right hand of God.

August 7, 2022

Ninth Sunday after Pentecost
Proper 14

Robin D. Dillon

Color

Green

Scripture Readings

Isaiah 1:1, 10-20; Psalm 50:1-8, 22-23;
Hebrews 11:1-3, 8-16; Luke 12:32-40

Theme Ideas

Eschatology focuses this week's readings, as we contemplate the coming of God's reign. Isaiah warns that God is not pleased with hollow worship and sacrifice. One must be cleansed by ceasing to do evil and by seeking justice. Likewise, the psalmist proclaims that salvation will be given to those whose sacrifice is praise and thanksgiving. In Hebrews, we are reminded of our ancestors' faith in things unseen, and of their hope in that which is yet to come. Luke tells us that God takes pleasure in opening God's realm to us. We must be alert, therefore, and ready to take action. God's reign is both here already, and not yet fully realized. Such is the challenge of faith.

Invitation and Gathering

Centering Words (Luke 12:32 AU)

Do not be afraid, little ones. It is God's pleasure to give you the kingdom.

Call to Worship (Psalm 50, Hebrews 11)

God called Abraham and Sarah
and promised to bless them.
> **Through faith they obeyed**
> **and received God's inheritance.**
God called Isaac and Jacob,
as heirs of that promise.
> **They too followed in faith,**
> **seeking God's realm.**
God calls us to join them,
as heirs with the faithful.
> **We come here in faith,**
> **assured by the hope that was fulfilled**
> **in the lives of your servants.**

Opening Prayer (Isaiah 1, Luke 12)

God of light and love,
> you take delight in your creation.
Ignite our spirits to worship you with sincerity.
Illumine our minds with the truth of your word.
Inspire our hearts to seek your treasure alone,
> that our hearts may be pure
> > and our actions may be noble and just,
> > > as we share your love.
Through Jesus Christ, our hope and promise,
> we pray. Amen.

Proclamation and Response

Prayer of Confession (Isaiah 1, Luke 12)

God of unfailing love, it is often hard to remain faithful.
You ask us to share our wealth with those in need,
   yet we hoard our possessions
      and guard our wealth.
You call us to rescue the oppressed,
   defend the orphan, and plead for the widow,
      yet our pursuits are often self-serving,
         ignoring those in need of our care.
Forgive us and cleanse us, O God.
Move us to be a people of justice,
   and propel us on the path of love. Amen.

Words of Assurance (Isaiah 1, Luke 12)

Though our sins are like scarlet, do not be afraid,
   for God has washed us clean.
The Lord takes pleasure in opening God's realm to us.
Rejoice and come in!

Passing the Peace of Christ (Luke 12)

Through Christ, God's realm has been opened to us.
Here and now, we enter this realm when we offer signs
of love and peace to one another. Greet one another in
the name of the Lord.

Introduction to the Word (Isaiah 1, Luke 12)

Listen for the word of God. Strive to understand Christ's
teachings. For this indeed is our treasure. May it light
our paths and make us ready to take action.

Response to the Word (Luke 12, Hebrews 11)

God, you come to us at unexpected times
    and in unexpected places.
With our lamps lit, we will walk by faith. Amen.

Thanksgiving and Communion

Offering Prayer (Isaiah 1, Luke 12)

Generous God, you offer us unfailing treasure in heaven.
In love and gratitude for your gifts to us,
    we return these gifts and offerings to you.
Use them and stretch them to ease the plight
    of the poor and the widow,
        the orphan and the downtrodden.
Use and stretch us,
    that we may do good, seek justice,
        and be your light in the world. Amen.

Sending Forth

Benediction (Luke 12, Hebrews 11)

Go forth in faith with your lamps lit,
    dressed for action.
Through us, Christ offers love to the world.
Go forth to be a blessings to everyone you meet.

August 14, 2022

Tenth Sunday after Pentecost
Proper 15
Mary Scifres

Color

Green

Scripture Readings

Isaiah 5:1-7; Psalm 80:1-2, 8-19; Hebrews 11:29–12:2; Luke 12:49-56

Theme Ideas

Today's readings highlight the unexpected truth of lives of faith: Destruction happens. Division happens. Faith does not always yield happy endings. Whichever passage we focus on today, we discover that faith does not yield a predictable or "happily ever after" ending. But it does require perseverance, as we move forward with God—even when moving forward with God divides us from those who are on different journeys, endangers our lives along the path, or even leaves us in a barren wilderness awaiting life and salvation. Perhaps this is why resurrection is such an important aspect of the Christian journey. The reality is this: Death comes. Destruction comes. Division comes. Hope arises in the miracle that life goes on anyway. New life emerges. Resurrection calls us to start again every time death comes to call.

Invitation and Gathering

Centering Words (Isaiah 5, Hebrews 12, Luke 12)

As the ancients remind us, we are surrounded by a great cloud of witnesses. Life is around us, even in the memories of ghosts and loved ones long gone. Death is but the other side of the coin of life. Hope is but the other side of the coin of despair. Unity is but the other side of the coin of division. Flip a coin. Choose your side. For life and hope await us on the other side.

Call to Worship (Isaiah 55, Luke 12)

In the fire and the flames,
> **Spirit appears to bless and inspire us.**

In the division and the despair,
> **Christ arrives to challenge and invite us.**

In the shadows and the sorrow,
> **God walks alongside to lift us up.**

In this moment, we gather together
to worship, to pray, to sing, and to lament.
> **We gather on this blessed journey**
> **of life, death, and resurrection.**

Opening Prayer (Luke 12)

Christ of mysterious paradox,
> enter the paradoxes of our lives.

Divide us when false unity divides us from you.

Unify us when false division separates us
    from one another.
Connect with us so securely,
    that we may connect with one another
        in the power of your Holy Spirit,
           as we worship together this day. Amen.

Proclamation and Response

Prayer of Confession (Isaiah 5, Luke 12)

Challenging Christ, forgive us when we avoid
    your hard truths.
Grant your mercy when we look for the easy path
    and avoid the path you set before us.
Guide us back to where you would have us go.
Strengthen us to face the challenge
    of living faithful lives
        and of following your lead.
Encourage us to rejoice when we see the way forward,
    and love us so fully that we accept your love.
Help us live the love you shower on our lives,
    that we may shower this love on others.
In your love and grace, we pray. Amen.

Words of Assurance (Psalm 80)

God's face looks upon us with mercy and love.
Christ's light shines through us as the image of God
    we are created to be.

Passing the Peace of Christ (Luke 12)

The peace of Christ is not an easy peace. This is not just
a peace of embracing those we love. This is a peace of
facing hard truths, forgiving huge sins, and uniting with

antagonists across great divides. Let us extend to one another the peace that Christ has extended to us.

Response to the Word

What if we were to lay aside the sin
of thinking we know everything?
What if we were to quit wishing
that the journey was simple and easy?
What if we were to accept division among us,
even in the midst of our unity?
What if we were to acknowledge sliding backward,
even as we move forward?
Christ Jesus, journey with us.
Hold us when we are afraid.
Lift us when we fall.
Push us forward when we would turn back.
Help us persevere and walk with you,
no matter what the journey brings.

Thanksgiving and Communion

Offering Prayer (Isaiah 5, Luke 12)

We praise you for your mighty and abundant love.
Sing through the gifts we return to you,
that others may know your great love.
Sing through our lives,
that through us, others may discover your song.
Sing through even our division,
that we may discover a unity
we have never tasted before
in your peace. Amen.

Sending Forth

Benediction (Luke 5)

We, who were far away, have been brought near
    in the grace of Christ.
We, who were once divided, have discovered peace
    in the unity of God's Spirit.
We, who were once alone, are connected
    in the love of God.
We, who were once lone individuals,
    are united as one body, one family of God ,
    to share God's unifying love with the world.

August 21, 2022

Eleventh Sunday after Pentecost
Proper 16

James Dollins

Color

Green

Scripture Readings

Jeremiah 1:4-10; Psalm 71:1-6; Hebrews 12:18-29;
Luke 13:10-17

Theme Ideas

In today's scriptures, God dignifies the very lives we tend to undervalue. Jesus heals a crippled woman, showing that God is not content to wait while someone suffers, even if it is the sabbath. Young Jeremiah, who doubts his own qualifications, learns that God has called and equipped him for great things. The psalmist feels assured of God's blessing, even from the beginning of life. We are all worthy of God's affections. May we treat ourselves and our neighbors accordingly.

Invitation and Gathering

Centering Words (Jeremiah 1, Psalm 71, Luke 13)

Just when we're about to dismiss ourselves or someone else, Jesus dignifies our lives with a touch, with healing power, and with the assurance that God is very near.

Call to Worship (Psalm 71)

In you, O God, I take refuge.
Let me never be put to shame.
In your righteousness, deliver me and rescue me.
Incline your ear to me, and save me!
For you, O Lord, are my hope,
my trust, O Lord, from my youth.
Upon you have I leaned from my birth.
It was you who took me from my mother's womb.
Your praise is continually on my lips.

Opening Prayer (Jeremiah 1, Luke 13)

Come, dear Christ, into this house of worship
and into every longing heart.
Some who gather here need healing.
Touch us, and give us strength.
Many feel confused by the news of the day.
Quiet our minds, and help us place our trust in you.
Many of us doubt ourselves and question our purpose.
Call us anew to be instruments of your grace
for a world that yearns to know your peace. Amen.

Proclamation and Response

Prayer of Confession (Jeremiah 1, Luke 13)

God of grace, we confess our uncertainty.
We are unsure of ourselves,
    so we cease to take risks.
We feel uncertain whom we should serve,
    so we neglect to serve those who are before us.
In seasons of doubt, we grow uncertain
    that you are even with us to guide us.
Awaken us to your presence,
    and renew us by your grace. Amen.

Words of Assurance (Psalm 71)

Truly, God is our hope, our trust, even from our birth.
In the name of Jesus Christ, we are forgiven.
Amen.

Response to the Word (Jeremiah 1, Luke 13)

God is not content to let us suffer.
Christ is unwilling to see us walk through life bent over,
excluded, and ashamed.
May God's Spirit touch you, heal you,
and make you whole.
    We will heed God's call in our lives,
    that we may bless those God sends us forth
    to serve.

Thanksgiving

Invitation to the Offering (Jeremiah 1, Luke 13)

The Spirit of God works through us, speaking hope through our words. The mercy of Christ works within us, healing neighbors through our actions in Christ's name. Now let us freely give of our time, treasure, and talent for the work of God's church in the world.

Offering Prayer (Psalm 71)

Generous God, you have blessed us
throughout our lives.
Take these offerings, and every gift we give,
and use them to show others
the breadth of your unfailing love. Amen.

Sending Forth

Benediction (Isaiah 43, John 12)

Stand tall and walk in Christ's peace.
Speak up and tell of God's goodness.
Touch and heal with the Spirit's love,
today and always. Amen.

August 28, 2022

Twelfth Sunday after Pentecost
Proper 17
Mary Scifres

Copyright © Mary Scifres

Color

Green

Scripture Readings

Jeremiah 2:4-13; Psalm 81:1, 10-16,
Hebrews 13:1-8, 15-16; Luke 14:1, 7-14

Theme Ideas

Hospitality, and the call to offer hospitality to strangers
and neighbors, flow through both Hebrews 13 and Luke
14. Even Jeremiah's judgment against the Israelites heralds back to that lost value of being God's people, caring
for the least, and welcoming the outcast. These transgressions lead to the Israelites becoming outcast in exile.
Until we remember and pursue these values, we run the
risk of being both lost and least. But when we embrace
these values, we become the hosts and community of
mutual love—the community of love Jesus envisions his
followers to be.

Invitation and Gathering

Centering Words (Hebrews 13)

Let mutual love continue, as it gathers your family and friends close. Let mutual love increase, as it extends to the stranger, the lost, and the lonely.

Call to Worship (Hebrews 13, Luke 14)

With gifts of praise,
> **we come to worship.**

With heartfelt prayers,
> **we come to worship and pray.**

With open minds, eager to grow,
> **we come to worship and grow this day.**

Opening Prayer or Response to the Word (Hebrews 13, Luke 14)

Loving God, flow through our worship and our lives.
Expand your love in and through each of us
and through our community of faith,
that we might create a house
of such hospitality and love
that all may feel truly welcome.
Reach out through each of us
and through our community of faith,
that we might reach out beyond our walls
to the stranger, the lost, and the lonely,
and that we might discover how abundant
your love truly is. Amen.

Proclamation and Response

Prayer of Confession (Hebrews 13, Luke 14, Jeremiah 2, Psalm 81)

God of love and grace, flow through our messy lives
with your abundant grace.
When we would close our hearts and doors,
open us to share your grace with others.
When we would neglect the needs of your world,
forgive us so abundantly
that we might be moved to give as abundantly
as we have received.
When we let pride and self-interest rule our days,
forgive us so miraculously
that we might live with humility and selflessness.
In your abundant love and miraculous grace,
may your world come to know your ways. Amen.

Words of Assurance (Psalm 81, Hebrew 13)

Like honey from a rock, Christ's love flows within us
with the sweetness of God's grace.
Like finest wheat, the Spirit's sustenance feeds us
with mercy and hope.
Thanks be to God!

Passing the Peace of Christ (Hebrews 13, Luke 14)

As we exchange signs of peace and love with one another, let us first look for the stranger who might one
day be our friend. Let us offer signs of peace and love
beyond the familiar friends we so often greet.

Response to the Word (Hebrews 13, Luke 14)

(You may begin with the Centering Words and then ask the following questions, with a time of silence for reflection following each question.)

Who is God calling you to help?

What stranger is in need of your welcome?

Who might you invite to worship next week?

Where might you continue and expand mutual love?

Thanksgiving and Communion

Offering Prayer (Luke 14)

Generous God, bless the gifts we return to you now,
that they may be gifts of abundance and grace
for a world in need. Amen.

Sending Forth

Benediction (Hebrews 13, Luke 14)

Go to share love with the world.

Go to invite the least and the lost.

Go to welcome the stranger.

Go to share love with the world.

September 4, 2022

Thirteenth Sunday after Pentecost
Proper 18

B. J. Beu

Color

Green

Scripture Readings

Jeremiah 18:1-11; Psalm 139:1-6, 13-18; Philemon 1-21;
Luke 14:25-33

Theme Ideas

Jeremiah and Psalm 139 communicate how intimately
God knows our individual and communal lives. Just as
a potter will rework a misshapen pot, so too will God
destroy Israel and fashion her anew if the people do
not repent. The psalmist celebrates God's knowledge of
our lives, even before we were born. And in the Gospel
reading, Jesus warns potential followers to know what
they are getting into. Disciples must count the cost before committing to life as his followers—foregoing their
possessions and relegating family obligations to a sec-
ondary status.

Invitation and Gathering

Centering Words (Jeremiah 18)

God is the potter; we are the clay. Rest in gratitude on the potter's wheel, for we are being shaped according to God's purposes. We are being molded into vessels of great beauty and infinite worth.

Call to Worship (Psalm 139)

When we try to hide,
God always finds us.
When we crawl into the darkness,
even there we don't escape God's eyes.
Are you tired of running from the one who loves you?
**We are here at last, ready and eager
to be made whole.**
Let us worship the living God.

Opening Prayer (Jeremiah 18)

O Lord, you are the potter,
we are the clay.
Take our lives, O God,
and remake us anew.
Pour out your Spirit upon us,
that we may be filled with living water.
Fit us for your purposes,
that we may be wholly yours. Amen.

Proclamation and Response

Prayer of Confession (Luke 14)

Holy God, we have sought to follow you
without counting the costs,
but our tanks are running empty
and we are afraid we can't go the distance.
We have hidden in the crowd,
ignoring Christ's call to pick up our cross
and follow him.
We have hidden in the stories we tell ourselves:
that we will attend to our spiritual walk some day—
just not this day.
Help us assess our motives and intentions,
even as we ponder our need for the journey.
For only then will we know
if we have what it takes
to finish the course in faith. Amen.

Assurance of Pardon (Jeremiah 18)

When we fall short in life,
God puts us on the potter's wheel
and fashions us into vessels fit for the kingdom.
This journey of transformation is rarely pleasant,
but it is necessary for us to be made new and whole.

Passing the Peace of Christ (Luke 12)

Christ calls us into service with him, but warns us to
count the cost before we put our shoulder to the plow.
Though the cost may seem high, the cost of trying to go
it alone is higher still. There is peace and ease in Christ's
yoke. Let us share this peace with one another.

Introduction to the Word (Psalm 139)

When we try to hide, Lord,
>you can always find us.
Even when we crawl into the darkness,
>we cannot escape your eyes.
We are tired of running, Lord.
We are here at last.
Share your teachings of life and death,
>for you love us as your people,
>>and we love you as our God. Amen.

Response to the Word (Psalm 139)

O Lord, you know us completely.
You discern our thoughts from far away.
>**You are acquainted with all our ways.**
>**Such knowledge is too wonderful for us.**
It is so high we cannot attain it.
>**You formed our inward parts,**
>**and knit us together in our mothers' wombs.**
We are fearfully and wonderfully made.
>**May we never take your blessings for granted,**
>**and may we never forget the depth of your love.**
Amen.

Thanksgiving and Communion

Offering Prayer (Jeremiah 18)

Loving Potter, you are ever mindful of your people.
You fashion us into vessels fit for your service,
>and transform our gifts and offerings,
>>into vessels to serve your world well.
You are worthy of our praise and glory. Amen.

Sending Forth

Benediction (Psalm 139, Jeremiah 18)
The one who shaped us in our mothers' wombs
loves and shapes us still.
God is the potter; we are the clay.
The one who formed our inward parts
continues to create us anew each and every day.
God is the potter; we are the clay.
The one who molds us in God's own image,
fashions us for glory.
God is the potter; we are the clay.
Go with God's blessings.

September 11, 2022

Fourteenth Sunday after Pentecost
Proper 19

Mary Scifres

Color

Green

Scripture Readings

Jeremiah 4:11-12, 22-28; Psalm 14; 1 Timothy 1:12-17; Luke 15:1-10

Theme Ideas

The surprise of grace is amazing indeed. Even as it seems absent from Jeremiah's words of doom, we know that Jeremiah will later proclaim hope to those God is sending into exile. Similarly, Luke's parable tells of a shepherd foolish enough with love for a lost sheep that he will risk the safety and security of the other ninety-nine in order to find the single lost soul. This is the surprise of grace: a judgmental, cruel Pharisee becomes an apostle of Christ's church; a sinful people will be welcomed back by their loving God; and a foolish sheep will be sought and found by the good shepherd, even as the obedient sheep are left behind untended. This isn't just surprising grace, this is foolish, illogical love—a love that only makes sense in God's realm.

Invitation and Gathering

Centering Words (Jeremiah 4, Psalm 14, 1 Timothy 1, Luke 15)

Return to God, no matter how long you've been away. Come home, no matter how far you've wandered. But if you don't return on your own, don't be surprised if God comes and finds you anyway. That's what we call grace.

Call to Worship (Jeremiah 4, Luke 15)

From our wanderings and wonderings,
we are welcomed home by God.
Lost on the highway or trapped on a cliff,
God comes to rescue and return us to safety.
Come to be found,
for all are welcome here.

Opening Prayer (Jeremiah 4, 1 Timothy 1, Luke 15)

Shepherding God,
gather us into your presence,
as we come to worship this day.
Transform us into your people
through the mighty power of your Spirit.
Rescue us with your endless patience,
that we may become instruments
of mercy and grace
to help others find their way home.
In your mercy and grace, we pray. Amen.

Proclamation and Response

Prayer of Yearing (Jeremiah 4, 1 Timothy 1, Luke 15)

Mighty One, be with us in our time of need.
Renew us with your fiery Spirit.
Love us with your endless patience.
Shelter us with your amazing grace.
Cleanse us with your refiner's fire
    and make us whole.
For this grace and mercy,
    we are more than grateful. Amen.

–Or–

Prayer of Confession (1 Timothy 1, Luke 15)

Loving Shepherd, pour your grace upon us this day.
Seek those who are wandering and lost,
    for they too need your grace.
For you know when we are wandering,
    and you know when we are lost.
You know when we have sinned,
    and when we have forsaken your call.
Forgive us, and bring us home.
Reclaim us and make us your own.
For you are our shepherd
    and we are the sheep of your pasture.
For this grace and mercy, we are ever grateful. Amen.

Words of Assurance (Psalm 14, Luke 15)

Rejoice, God has changed our circumstances
    for the better!
Christ's mercy and grace redeem us
    and bring us home.
We who were lost have been found.

Passing the Peace of Christ (Luke 15)

In grace, we are welcomed home. In grace, let us welcome one another home with signs of peace and love.

Response to the Word (Psalm 14, 1 Timothy 1, Luke 15)

The shepherd is searching,
that all may be found.
Grace is flowing,
that all may find their way home.
Love is waiting,
to welcome us into the arms of God.
(This litany flows nicely into the prayer below.)

Prayer of Response or Prayer of Thanksgiving (Psalm 14, 1 Timothy 1, Luke 15)

Loving God, our hearts are filled with your joy.
Thank you for welcoming us home.
Thank you for finding us when we are lost,
and for gathering us into the arms of your love
and your amazing grace.

Thanksgiving and Communion

Offering Prayer (1 Timothy 1, Luke 15)

Thank you, generous God of grace,
for pouring your love and abundance
so freely upon us.
Pour this same love and abundance
upon the gifts we now return to you,
that they may become signs of grace
and instruments of love
to bring the world back home to you.
Amen.

Invitation to Communion (Jeremiah 4, Psalm 14, 1 Timothy 1, Luke 15)

J. R. R. Tolkien once wrote, "Not all those who wander are lost." In Christ's love, even when we wander, we are never truly lost. We are found by the grace of God. And since we all wander, we all depend on such grace. Here, we come to the table of grace, where all are welcome, no matter how far we have wandered or how lost we feel. Here, we are welcomed home.

Sending Forth

Benediction (Jeremiah 4, 1 Timothy 1, Luke 15)

Found by God,
> **we go now to help others find their way.**

Loved by Christ,
> **we go now to share Christ's love with the world.**

Blessed by the Spirit,
> **we go now to bless others with mercy and grace.**

September 18, 2022

Fifteenth Sunday after Pentecost
Proper 20

B. J. Beu

Copyright © B. J. Beu

Color

Green

Scripture Readings

Jeremiah 8:18–9:1; Psalm 79:1-9; 1 Timothy 2:1-7;
Luke 16:1-13

Theme Ideas

Stewardship is a natural way to focus these readings.
While Jeremiah and the psalmist cry out to God for help
in the midst of Israel's distress, there is much that faith
communities can do to ease the suffering of others. In
Luke, Jesus tells a perplexing parable about a dishonest steward who, after being fired for mismanaging his
master's accounts, acts shrewdly to ingratiate himself
to those who owe his master money. Jesus challenges
the children of light to be as wise in spiritual matters as
this dishonest steward is with earthly matters. Proper

management of our time, talents, and treasure matters—
for if we cannot be trusted to be good stewards of dishonest wealth, how can God trust us to be faithful stewards of spiritual riches?

Invitation and Gathering

Centering Words (Luke 16)

You are far more talented than you give yourself credit
for. Be faithful in what you have been given, and God
will bless you with more. But be unfaithful in what you
have been given, and God will take it away. May we,
who are asked to give an accounting of our talents, be
found faithful.

Call to Worship (Jeremiah 8, Psalm 79)

Is God not in Zion?

Is there no ruler to lead us?

Search for the Lord,

for God waits where we least expect it.

Is there no balm in Gilead?

Is there no healer to help us?

Cry out to the Lord,

for God hears our pleas.

Is there no hope left to be found?

Is there nowhere to turn?

Place your trust in the Lord,

whose compassion comes speedily to meet us.

Come, worship the one who hears our pleas.

We will enter God's gates

with hope and gladness.

Opening Prayer (Jeremiah 8:22, Psalm 79)

Elusive One, the scoffers say,
  "Is there no balm in Gilead?
  Is there no physician there?"
Why do you tarry when your people need you?
Why do you hide your face when our need is great?
Speed your compassion to our side,
  for our souls have become wellsprings of sorrow,
    and our eyes have become rivers of tears.
Help us, O God of our salvation,
  for in you alone do we find our strength
    to revive our souls;
  in you alone do we find nourishment
    to meet the needs for the journey.
Come speedily to us once more,
  that we may see your glory
    and know where our true help lies. Amen.

Proclamation and Response

Prayer of Yearning (Jeremiah 8, Psalm 79, 1 Timothy 2, Luke 16)

Holy One, in the midst of life's travails,
  be once more the balm in Gilead
    that makes the wounded whole;
  become for us the healing balm
    that heals the sin-sick soul.
For we are weary in body and tired in soul,
  as we strive to live faithfully as children of light—
    children who are wise
      in the ways of your kingdom.

Too often, we neglect the talents you give us,
    and act less shrewdly with your true riches
        than the unscrupulous do
            with the dishonest wealth of this world.
As you search our hearts and ways,
    may we be found faithful in a little,
        that you will entrust us to be faithful in much.
Amen.

Assurance of Pardon (Jeremiah 8, Psalm 79)

Rejoice and be glad,
    for even when sorrow grips us,
    God's compassion comes speedily to meet us.
Be still and know that there is a balm in Gilead
    that heals the sin-sick soul.

Passing the Peace of Christ (1 Timothy 2)

When we offer supplications, prayers, intercessions, and thanksgiving for others, we discover Christ's peace—a peace that passes all understanding. Let us share signs of this peace with one another.

Response to the Word (Luke 16)

God has made us stewards of true riches
    that we may live and work tirelessly
    as children of light.
May we be found faithful in what we have received,
    that God will bless us abundantly,
    as we work to bring the kingdom of God
    into our midst.

Thanksgiving and Communion

Offering Prayer (Luke 16)

Source of every good gift,
> you call us to be wise with the true riches
> > of your kingdom

May this offering show such wisdom,
> that having been found faithful in a little,
> > you will trust us to be faithful in much.

We offer you these gifts in gratitude for your love,
> that they may bring healing and light
> > to those who need your balm of Gilead. Amen.

Sending Forth

Benediction (Luke 16)

Be faithful in a little,
> that you may also be found faithful in much.

Be faithful in much,
> that you may be entrusted with the true riches
> that come from above.

Go to be faithful children of light,
> and come to know the grace, hope, and peace
> of the one who is truly faithful.

September 25, 2022

Sixteenth Sunday after Pentecost
Proper 21

Mary Scifres

Copyright © Mary Scifres

Color

Green

Scripture Readings

Jeremiah 32:1-3a, 6-15; Psalm 91:1-6, 14-16;
1 Timothy 6:6-19; Luke 16:19-31

Theme Ideas

Today's scripture readings share a similar message: our earthly situations do not have the last word. The rich man may suffer a horrible fate. The exiled people are invited to buy houses and fields and look to a day of redemption. The person in danger is still sheltered by God's faithful presence. Timothy speaks it most plainly: "Be rich in good works . . . that [you] may take hold of the life that really is life" (1 Tim 6:18-19 NRSV) By embracing what is truly life, the goodness of God flowing through us, we connect to that which is eternal, rather than our temporary earthly situations.

Invitation and Gathering

Centering Words (1 Timothy 6:18a, 19b CEB Adapted)
Be rich in the good things you do, that you may take hold of what is truly life.

Call to Worship (Jeremiah 32, Psalm 91)
Sheltered by God,
>**we come now to worship.**

Invited by Christ,
>**we come now to pray.**

Welcomed by the Spirit,
>**we gather as the people of God.**

Opening Prayer (Psalm 91)
Sheltering God, as we worship you this day,
>cover us with the presence of your Holy Spirit.

Gather us in the goodness of your grace,
>that we may experience your comforting presence
>>and your powerful protection.

In your loving name, we pray. Amen.

Proclamation and Response

Prayer of Confession (Psalm 91, Luke 16)
O God, you are our refuge in times of trouble,
>our shelter in times of rain.

When we forget to be refuge for others in trouble,
>forgive us.

Turn our gaze to the poor Lazaruses of our world,
>for we would rather look away.

Guide our lives to be places of shelter for others,
>as you have been shelter for us.

Strengthen us with your grace,
that we may offer our mercy and help to the needy,
as you have offered your mercy and help to us.
Draw us back into the protection
of your forgiveness and grace.
In hope and gratitude, we pray. Amen.

Words of Assurance (Psalm 91, Luke 16)
Because we have called, God has answered.
We are delivered and saved by God's love.

Introduction to the Word (1 Timothy 6)
As we listen to the words of life,
may they inspire us to pursue righteousness,
holy living, faithfulness, love, endurance,
and gentleness.

Response to the Word
May we be rich in good things:
attending to the poor
and caring for those in need.
May we be generous with our lives:
giving treasure and time
to make this world a better place.
May we take hold of what is truly life,
the goodness of God flowing in and through us.

Thanksgiving and Communion

Offering Prayer (1 Timothy 6, Luke 16)

Generous God, open our hearts and our wallets
  to be as generous with others as you are with us.
Bless the gifts we offer to you,
  that they may be gifts of generous love for others.
May we be generous givers
  of our time, talent, treasure, and service,
    that others may find in us
      generous and loving friends.
In gratitude and joy, we pray. Amen.

Invitation to Communion (Psalm 91, 1 Timothy 6, Luke 16)

This is a table where all are welcome:
  the poor and the rich,
  the righteous and the sinful,
  the courageous and the timid.
Whether you have wandered far or remained close,
  Christ invites you to this table of grace,
    this abundant feast of love for all.

Sending Forth

Benediction (Psalm 91)

God be with you in the week ahead.
In times of trouble, in times of joy,
  may God be your refuge and strength;
  may Christ be the foundation of your life.

October 2, 2022

Seventeenth Sunday after Pentecost
World Communion Sunday
Proper 22
B. J. Beu

Color

Green

Scripture Readings

Lamentations 1:1-6; Psalm 137; 2 Timothy 1:1-14;
Luke 17:5-10

Theme Ideas

These readings stand as a warning to those who believe
that faith ensures prosperity. Certainly, not everyone
in Judah forsook the Lord when Babylon and the surrounding nations destroyed the holy city of Jerusalem
and sent her people into exile. Lamentations and Psalm
137 speak of tears, groans, distress, and unremitting suffering for a people used to fine pastures and the joys of
God's delights. Second Timothy makes clear that Paul's
suffering is a result of preaching the gospel of Jesus

Christ—the gospel of power and grace. Sharing the truth is its own reward. Finally, Christ warns his disciples that those who labor in the fields cannot expect to come in and dine when their work is done. They must first go to prepare the meal for the master of the house. Working for the gospel is its own reward, and those who do so should not expect special dispensations of earthly ease and comfort. But when we forsake earthly comforts to guard the good treasure entrusted to us, the Holy Spirit helps us in our time of need.

Invitation and Gathering

Centering Words (Luke 17)

Christians around the world gather this day to share holy communion as one body—a body united in the love and mercy of Christ. We gather with them, rejoicing in our unity in Christ.

Call to Worship (Lamentations 1, Psalm 137, 2 Timothy 2)

When we feel spiritually homeless,
where can we turn for help?
Our help is in the grace of God.
When we are imprisoned in our suffering,
where can we turn for solace?
Our solace is in the mercy of Christ.
When we are trapped in the grip of misfortune,
where can we turn for strength?
Our strength is in the power of the Holy Spirit.
Come! Let us worship God, our guide and guardian.

Opening Prayer (Lamentations 1, Psalm 137, 2 Timothy 2)

Merciful God, though you often feel far from us,
>   you meet us in our need.
When our mouths know the taste of bitter tears,
>   you bring us to the feast of your love and mercy.
When grief threatens to steal our joy,
>   you remind us to sing of happier times.
When adversaries enjoy our misfortune,
>   you rekindle the hope that lies hidden within us.
When fear robs us of our courage,
>   you fill us with the daring to begin anew.
Be with us in this time of worship,
>   that we may be brought back to life,
>   through the grace of your Son,
>   who walks with us in the journey of faith.
Amen.

Proclamation and Response

Prayer of Yearning (Lamentations 1, 2 Timothy 1)

God of eternal return, in times of bitter loss,
>   we yearn to be called home.
How often have we felt like exiles of Israel
>   who sat down by the waters of Babylon
>   to weep at all they had lost?
How often have we felt like Paul
>   who was persecuted and locked away
>   for his convictions and beliefs?
Yet we cringe at Paul's invitation
>   to join him in suffering for the gospel.

We want to pick up our cross
>and be counted among the faithful,
>>but we can't seem to leave our hurts behind.
>Help us be the people you call us to be,
>>and give us the courage to follow you anew
>>>in the power and strength of your loving Spirit.
Amen.

Words of Assurance (2 Timothy 1)

Even in our doubt,
>God gives us a spirit of power, love,
>and self-discipline.
Even in our failure to find meaning,
>Christ gives us the gospel of truth.
Even in our despair,
>the Spirit gives us treasure from heaven
>to strengthen us on our way.
Rejoice in the mercy of our God.

Passing the Peace of Christ (2 Timothy 1)

Grandmothers like Lois, and mothers like Eunice, are here in midst to nurture us in our faith. Teachers like Paul reside in our fellowship to share the gospel with us. Students like Timothy are among us, looking for guidance. See them in the faces around you, as you pass the peace of Christ with one another this day.

Response to the Word (2 Timothy 1, Luke 17)

Hold fast to the teaching you have received
>through the Spirit of wisdom and truth.
Hold true to the faith and love you have been given
>through Christ Jesus.
Guard the treasure of new life in Christ
>through the help of the Spirit living within you.

Thanksgiving and Communion

Offering Prayer (Psalm 137)

You call us to bloom where we are planted, O God,
> even when we feel like strangers in a foreign land.

You invite us to play instruments and sing songs of joy,
> even when our hearts are heavy,
>> and our spirits cry out in anguish.

God of tender mercy,
> you alone can turn our tears of sadness
>> into tears of joy.

May the gifts we bring before you this day
> turn groans of despair into shouts of mirth
>> and gladness.

Bless this offering with your abundant power,
> that the world may know your grace
>> and find life in the midst of death. Amen.

Communion Litany

With Christians around the world,
come to the festival of love.
> **We come with thanksgiving and praise.**

With believers from every continent on earth,
come to the festival of grace.
> **We come with thanksgiving and praise.**

With the whole body of Christ,
come to the festival of life.
> **We come with thanksgiving and praise.**

(From B. J. Beu and Mary Scifres, *Is It Communion Sunday Already?! Communion Resources for All Seasons*)

The Great Thanksgiving

The Lord be with you.
> **And also with you.**

Lift up your hearts.
> **We lift them up to the Lord.**

Let us give thanks to the Lord, our God.
> **It is right to give our thanks and praise.**

It is right, and a good and joyful thing,
> always and everywhere, to give thanks to you,
> Almighty God, creator of all things in heaven
> and on earth.

In the beginning, you brought forth life,
> that every living thing might live in harmony
> in the great circle of life.

After fashioning our frame from the dust
> and bones of the earth,
> you placed your image within us,
> and declared that it was not good for us to be alone.

Created to be in unity and harmony with creation
> and with one another,
> you sent us prophets and teachers
> when we broke fellowship with one another
> and when our pride sought out differences among us.

In the fullness of time, you sent your Son, Jesus Christ,
> to fashion us into a holy community
> that would be his body here on earth.

Even when dissent and division
> threatened to pull his followers apart,
> Jesus prayed that we might all be one in his name,
> and shared with us the bread of heaven
> and the cup of our salvation in his name.

And so, with your people on earth,
    and all the company of heaven,
    we praise your name
    and join their unending hymn, saying,
    Holy, holy, holy Lord, God of power and might,
        heaven and earth are full of your glory.
    Hosanna in the highest.
    Blessed is the one who comes
        in the name of the Lord.
    Hosanna in the highest.

Holy are you, and blessed is your bread of heaven,
    Christ Jesus.
When you sent Christ to be with us,
    he offered his very self,
    that we might have the strength to stand
    when all hope seems lost.
Through the holy mystery of this table,
    you invite us into your presence,
    tend us in our weakness,
    and strengthen us through this bread and cup.

With joy and gratitude, we remember that night
    when Jesus took the bread, broke it,
    and gave it to his disciples, saying,
    "Take, eat, this is the bread of life, given for you.
    Do this in remembrance of me."
After supper, Jesus took the cup, blessed it,
    and gave it to his disciples, saying,
    "Drink from this, all of you.
    This is my life in the new covenant,
    poured out for you and for many
    for the forgiveness of sins.

Do this, as often as you drink it,
in remembrance of me."

And so, in remembrance of these,
your mighty acts of love and grace,
we offer ourselves in praise and thanksgiving.
As your covenant people
and as reflections of your glory,
in union with Christ's love for us,
we proclaim the mystery of faith.
Christ has died.
Christ is risen.
Christ will come again.
(From Beu and Scifres, *Is It Communion Sunday Already?!*)

Sending Forth

Benediction (World Communion Sunday)
With Christians around the world,
go forth to bear witness in a divided and broken world.
Knit together in Christian love,
we leave here to share living bread
with a world starving for spiritual food.
With Christians around the world,
go forth blessed through fellowship with Christ
to be in union with God and the Holy Spirit.
Woven together in Christian hope,
we leave to share the cup of salvation
with a world dying of thirst.

October 9, 2022

Eighteenth Sunday after Pentecost
Proper 23
B. J. Beu

Color

Green

Scripture Readings

Jeremiah 29:1, 4-7; Psalm 66:1-12; 2 Timothy 2:8-15;
Luke 17:11-19

Theme Ideas

Suffering is a part of life. It's how we respond that shows
us who we are. Do we give up or do we push through?
Do we curse those who curse us or do we bless them?
Jeremiah tells the exiles in Babylon to build houses,
plant gardens, and pray for the welfare of the city where
they are held captive—for their welfare is found in the
city's welfare. The psalmist notes that God has tested
the people with fire and water, but God has also brought
them out to a spacious place. The proper response to
such grace is worship and praise. Paul tells Timothy

that while he is chained for the gospel, the word of God is not, and that he embraces his suffering gladly for the sake of God's elect. After healing ten lepers, Jesus remarks that only one leper is truly made well—for only one returns to give thanks. Suffering happens. That's life. But how we respond to this suffering makes all the difference in the world.

Invitation and Gathering

Centering Words (Jeremiah 29, Luke 17)

Are you stuck in the past? Have you lost hope for the future? Do not despair. Build houses of joy. Plant gardens of faith. Offer thanks and praise to the living God. All will be well.

Call to Worship (Psalm 66, Luke 17)

Sing God's praises.
Make a joyful noise to the Lord.
We have walked through fire and water
with heavy burdens on our backs.
But God has led us into a spacious place
to plant gardens of faith.
Rejoice in the Lord.
Build houses of joy
and shout glory to our God.
Let us worship in gratitude and praise.

Opening Prayer (Jeremiah 29, 2 Timothy 2, Luke 17)

Master Gardener, you revive us
when our bodies grow weak,
and when our spirits faint within us.
Though we may be bound by our worries,
your word is not chained.
Help us build houses of joy
and plant gardens of faith.
As we pray for the welfare of our communities,
help us bloom where we are planted,
that your harvest of hope and love
may be bountiful.
In gratitude for your blessings, we pray. Amen.

Proclamation and Response

Prayer of Yearning (Jeremiah 29, Psalm 66)

Mysterious One, why does life seem like a test
we cannot endure?
Why have we been led into the net,
only to have burdens laid on our backs?
Why has our path led us through fire and water,
while others ride over our heads?
You have tried us like silver,
refined us like gold.
Still, our hearts rejoice in your presence.
For it was you who brought us through the wilderness
to a good and spacious place.
Though we do not understand your ways,
we will praise your name forever.
For you are our deepest desire,
our source of hope and deliverance. Amen.

Words of Assurance (2 Timothy 2)

Just as we have died with Christ,
    so shall we live with him.
And just as we have endured hardships with Christ,
    so shall we abide in his grace and mercy.

Passing the Peace of Christ (Jeremiah 29)

Christ calls us to seek the welfare of this place and to plant gardens of faith. May we do both as we share signs of Christ's peace with one another. For only in the peace of Christ can we flower as God's people.

Introduction to the Word (2 Timothy 2)

The word of God cannot be chained.
Let us listen for that word—
    for it proclaims grace and love;
    it heals our souls.

Response to the Word (2 Timothy 2, Luke 17)

Let us be doers of the word,
    and not hearers only.
Let us present ourselves to God as disciples of Christ,
    that we may be approved by the Holy Spirit,
    and share God's word of truth with the world.

Thanksgiving and Communion

Invitation to the Offering (Jeremiah 29)

Even in exile, God instructed the people to seek the welfare of the city that ripped them from their homes. No matter where and with whom we live, our welfare is tied to the welfare of others. Let us give generously, that we may plant the love of God through the ministries and missions of this church.

Offering Prayer (Psalm 66, Luke 17)

Author of life, you meet us in our need.
Your love and grace surround us.
When our world gets turned upside down,
    you carry us through the trials of life.
Your power gives us the strength to find healing
    and comfort each day.
Receive these gifts as signs of our thanks.
Accept our praise for your many blessings.
Receive our very lives,
    that we may serve you in the ministry
        of your church. Amen.

Sending Forth

Benediction (Jeremiah 29, Luke 17)

As you go forth this day, build houses of love
and plant gardens of faith.
    We will sow seeds of faith and hope,
    and bloom where we are planted.
Care for your neighbors,
and bear the fruit of kindness and compassion.
    We will grow in the power of God's Spirit,
    and bloom with the grace of Christ's love.
Go with God.

October 16, 2022

Nineteenth Sunday after Pentecost
Proper 24

Mary Scifres

Copyright © Mary Scifres

Color

Green

Scripture Readings

Jeremiah 31:27-34; Psalm 119:97-104; 2 Timothy 3:14–4:5;
Luke 18:1-8

Theme Ideas

Today, we focus on the power of prayer, and the power
of persistence and tenacity in prayer, as taught by Jesus's parable of the persistent widow in Luke 18. Those
looking for themes of God's guidance and teachings can
find resources in both the 2013 and 2016 editions of the
Abingdon Worship Annual. Today's resources, however,
focus on prayer alone.

Invitation and Gathering

Centering Words (1 Thessalonians 5, Luke 18)

Pray without ceasing. Pray without giving up.
Pray with tenacity, courage, and hope.

Call to Worship

Called by God to be people of prayer,
    we gather today as people of prayer.
Come, let us worship and pray together.

Opening Prayer (Luke 18)

Mighty God, we come into your powerful presence
    with hope in our hearts.
May we pray with the same focus and strength
    with which you receive our prayers.
Flow through our prayers and our worship this day,
    that we may rediscover childlike trust,
        even as we mature in faith. Amen.

Proclamation and Response

Prayer of Confession (Jeremiah 31, Luke 18)

Faithful God, when our prayers are absent,
    speak to us and return our attention to you.
When our prayers and attitudes are self-serving,
    humble us and bring us back
        to compassionate and caring ways.
God of faith and God of glory,
    give us confidence when our faith falters.
Empower us with your Spirit,
    that we may pray with confidence and faith,
        and with tenacity and courage,
            all the days of our lives. Amen.

Words of Assurance (Luke 18)

If an unjust judge will listens to the pleas
 of a persistent widow,
  how much more will our compassionate God
  listen to us when we pray?
God hears your prayers
 and answers with mercy and grace.
God's answer imprints love on our very hearts.
In this mercy and grace, we are given forgiveness,
 help, and sustenance.
Receive these gifts and rejoice, for all is well.

Passing the Peace of Christ (Luke 18)

Turn to your neighbor and silently offer a prayer of
peace and love:
 Peace and love be with you this day.

Response to the Word (Luke 18)

Pray without ceasing.
 Pray without giving up.
Pray with tenacity.
 Pray with courage.
Pray with hope.
 For God hears our every prayer.

Thanksgiving and Communion

Invitation to the Offering (Luke 18)

Even as God invites us to bring our needs in prayer, God
also invites us to bring our gifts in service to the world.
Let us bring our gifts with as much tenacity and courage
as we bring our needs and prayers before God.

Offering Prayer (Luke 18)

Mighty God, bestow your power and strength
   on these gifts we now return to you.
Multiply them as they go forth
   to serve your church and your world. Amen.

Sending Forth

Benediction (Jeremiah 31, Luke 18)

As people of prayer, go now to live your prayers.
As people of faith, go now to live in faith.
As people of love, go now to live with love.

October 23, 2022

Twentieth Sunday after Pentecost
Reformation Sunday
Proper 25

Joanne Carlson Brown

Color

Green

Scripture Readings

Joel 2:23-32; Psalm 65; 2 Timothy 4:6-8, 16-18;
Luke 18:9-14

Theme Ideas

God is indeed gracious to God's people. They will be
vindicated, restored, and without shame. But they
should not succumb to self-righteousness or to "diss-
ing" other people who, it may turn out, are more in right
relationship with God than they are.

Invitation and Gathering

Centering Words (Joel 2, Psalm, Luke 18)

Rejoice in the beauty of God's creation. God has blessed God's people with many gifts and promises, and we humbly thank our God.

Call to Worship (Joel 2, Psalm 65)

God has called our daughters and sons to gather,
old and young alike.
We are here to answer God's call.
Let us rejoice in the many gifts God has provided.
We are here to praise God's goodness.
Let us worship and praise God with all our might.

Opening Prayer (Joel 2, Psalm 65, Luke 18)

Amazing God, we come to give you thanks
for everything your people have received.
May we feel the joy our ancestors felt
at their vindication and restoration.
Open us to your call, to witness to your grace,
in the words and actions of our lives.
Help us pray without pride or guile,
that we may receive the greatest gift of all—
being in your presence forever and always.
Amen.

Proclamation and Response

Prayer of Confession (Joel 2, 2 Timothy, Luke 18)

We are here, O God, to worship and to pray.
We are here to give you thanks
for all you have given us.

Forgive us when we feel a bit proud
of our prayers and our actions as your people.
Remake us when we look down on the marginalized
and those who are different.
Help us see all people as your beloved ones
and act accordingly.
Help us truly be sons and daughters of your love,
who know what we are called to do
no matter our age or our circumstances.
Help us dream dreams of justice,
and then live those dreams into reality,
and we strive to be your beloved community.
When we take your gifts for granted,
help us run the race you set before us,
and help us work to make the world
what you created it to be.

Words of Assurance (Luke 18)

God hears our prayers
and receives our prayers lovingly.
God also receives us, just as we are,
into God's loving arms,
that we may feel safe and warm and cherished.
God hears our hearts and loves us for it.

Passing the Peace (Luke 18)

Sister/brother, claim your identity as a beloved one of
God.

Litany of Reformation

(We are not as clearly divided as we were in the Reformation but still there are things we feel we cannot compromise. What was meant to be a uniting sacrament has been the most

divisive thing in Christianity. As Protestants, we celebrate our freedom from theologies that no longer fit, church structures that seemed oppressive, and practices that seemed superstitious. As Catholics, we grieve the tearing apart of the church universal and the denigration of our beliefs and practices. What does the Reformation mean to us today?)

Once, we were one church under God.
> **But a tear was ripped in that fabric.**

People were in turmoil, not sure of what was true.
> **Confusion and deep convictions reigned.**

People were willing to die horrible deaths
for their beliefs.
> **How did it come to this: Wars of religion,**
> **torture, persecutions, intransigents?**

But through it all, people tried to worship
in the way they thought God wanted them to.
> **They were searching for truth**
> **when there are many truths and paths to God.**

We give thanks today for the courage of those
who stood for what they believed deeply in their hearts.
> **There are too many to name aloud here,**
> **but their names ring in the ears of God.**

On this Reformation Sunday, we pray for unity
in the midst of diversity of thought and understanding.
May God bless our remembrance,
and may God bless our work to respect all
who love and serve God in their own way.
> **We give thanks to God for the ancestors**
> **who paved the way for us to follow.**

Prayer of Preparation (Joel 2)

Empty the rushing of our minds, Holy One,
and the noise that blocks out your message.
Open our hearts and minds to the words
we are about to hear.
Seal them in our hearts.

Response to the Word (Joel 2, Psalm 65)

May we hear and respond to your word and teachings.
May we dream dreams and have visions
of what is possible through your aid and guidance.

Thanksgiving and Communion

Invitation to Offering (Joel 2, Psalm 65)

God has dealt wonderfully with us. We have what we need. Now we are called to share from our abundance to support the work of God through this church. May we give gladly, however great or small, to thank God for our call to be Christ's hands and feet in the world.

Offering Prayer (Joel 2)

God, we are so grateful that you name and claim us
as your beloved ones.
We thank you with all our hearts
for the cleansing rain in our souls.
And so we offer you what we have:
our resources, our time, our energy, our very selves
for your ministry in the world. Amen.

Sending Forth

Benediction

Go forth without shame
> to proclaim the goodness of God.

Go forth to spread God's love with all,
> giving thanks for how much you are loved.

Go forth, knowing that the wind of the Spirit
> blows you to where you need to be. Amen.

October 30, 2022

Twenty-First Sunday after Pentecost
Proper 26

B. J. Beu

Color

Green

Scripture Readings

Habakkuk 1:1-4; 2:1-4; Psalm 119:137-44;
2 Thessalonians 1:1-4, 11-12; Luke 19:1-10

Theme Ideas

Watching and waiting is central to the spiritual life. Facing injustice and abuse by the powerful, Habakkuk declares that he will watch and wait until God answers his petition for justice. In response to Habakkuk's vigil, God promises a vision that does not lie—a vision where the righteous will live by faith. Zacchaeus climbs a tree as he waits to see Jesus. In response, salvation comes to his house that day. The psalmist proclaims God's righteousness and delight in God's precepts.

Invitation and Gathering

Centering Words (Habakkuk 2)

Stand at your watchpost and wait for the Lord. A vision has been promised at the appointed time. It speaks of the end and does not lie. Stand at your watchpost and wait.

Call to Worship (Habakkuk 1, 2)

What will you do when the strong devour the weak, when cries of violence go unanswered?
We will stand at our watchposts
and wait for the Lord.
We will wait for a vision of hope and rescue.
What will you do when strife and contention arise, when the wicked pervert justice?
We will stand at our watchposts
and pray to the Lord.
We will pray for righteousness and mercy.
What will you do when the law becomes slack, when justice fails, and the land is bereft of peace?
We will stand at our watchposts
and hope in the Lord.
We will trust that God's justice will not tarry.
Stand at your watchposts and wait for the Lord.

–Or–

Call to Worship (Luke 19)

When we need to climb a tree to look for help, Christ proclaims,
"I am coming to your house today."
When we feel lost, and have nowhere to turn, Christ assures us,

"I am coming to your house today."
Christ is coming. Christ is with us even now.
Worship the Lord with joy and praise.

Opening Prayer or Prayer of Yearning (Habakkuk 1, Psalm 119, Luke 19)

Righteous One, hear our cries
in the bitter watches of the night.
We come before you with zeal in our hearts,
ready to stand at our watchposts,
ready to receive the vision you promise your people.
We come seeking justice for the weak,
hope for the downtrodden,
and healing for the afflicted.
In times of trial, we yearn to see your face,
and behold the glory of our salvation.
Be the vision we need,
that we may find the courage to persevere,
that salvation may come to our homes this day,
through the power of your Holy Spirit. Amen.

Proclamation and Response

Prayer of Yearning (Habakkuk 1, 2, Psalm 119, Luke 19)

God of promised vision, we await your word of hope.
As we stand at our watchposts,
come to us in our need,
for we are weary and heavy laden.
As we await your reply to our pleas for mercy,
respond to our longing for friendship,
for we are beaten down by hatred and violence.

Zeal for your endless love consumes us,
>even as we await the promise of our salvation.
Come to our homes this day,
>and abide in our hearts each hour,
>>through the glory of your Son. Amen.

Words of Assurance (Luke 19)

When all hope seemed lost,
>Christ came to save the weak and the outcast.
When justice lagged and righteousness ebbed,
>Christ came to save the hopeless and despondent.
Today, salvation has come to this house of worship,
>for in Christ, we are renewed and made whole,
>>through the power of the Holy Spirit.

Passing the Peace (2 Thessalonians 1:2)

Let us share God's grace, as we exchange signs of Christ's peace this day.

Response to the Word (Psalm 119, 2 Thessalonians 1, Luke 19)

Do not forget God's precepts.
>**God's righteousness is everlasting;**
>**God's teachings lead to life.**
With prayers of hope and songs of joy,
live God's word as people of promise.
>**Salvation has come to our homes this day,**
>**for Christ is our honored guest.**
With acts of grace and works of the Spirit,
share God's word as people of peace.

–Or–

Response to the Word (Habakkuk 2, Psalm 119)
With abiding love,
   sing glory to our God.
With expectant faithfulness,
   proclaim God's justice and righteousness.
With lasting peace,
   worship the God of our salvation.

Thanksgiving and Communion

Offering Prayer (Psalm 119, Luke 19)
God of many blessings,
   you come to us as Christ came to Zacchaeus,
     that salvation may come to our homes
       to show us the power of your love.
When we stand at the watchposts of our lives,
   you meet us to share a vision of hope and justice.
May the offering we bring before you now
   be a sign of our commitment to live your vision
     and to share your generosity with our world.
Come to us, abide in our homes,
   and work within these offerings,
     that all may know your love and justice.
Amen.

Sending Forth

Benediction (Habakkuk 1, 2, Luke 19)

Though the night of travail seems long,
and the time at your watchposts seems in vain,
God's vision of hope will not tarry.
Though hatred and violence hold sway,
and the strong devour the weak,
Christ's salvation is at hand.
Though the wicked surround the righteous,
and justice seems perverted,
the Spirit's truth heralds in the land.
Go with God's blessings.

November 1, 2022

All Saints Day

Mary Scifres and B. J. Beu

Color

White

Scripture Readings

Daniel 7:1-3, 15-18; Psalm 149; Ephesians 1:11-23;
Luke 6:20-31

Theme Ideas

The inheritance of the saints pervades today's scriptures, yet understanding this inheritance remains an
ongoing challenge. When facing death and remembrance, many find comfort in the idea that our inheritance is a heavenly home with God. Yet, the kingdom
we are promised is much more than a promised after-
life. Perhaps the inheritance is to praise God's glory,
both now and forevermore, as Ephesians 1:12 suggests.
Perhaps the inheritance is actual growth in godliness
and humility, that we might be one with those whom
Jesus calls blessed. Paul prays that God may give us a
spirit of wisdom and revelation, as we grow in our love

and knowledge of Christ, and as we lead others on this journey. In this growth, we discern the hope to which we are called, the hope that called those who came before us. All Saints Day is a perfect occasion to lift up those who have died in the faith.

Invitation and Gathering

Centering Words (Psalm 149)

Rejoice and be glad, for the Lord reigns. God lifts up the lowly, and casts down the mighty. The Lord adorns the humble with victory, and visits judgment upon the proud. Rejoice and be glad, for truly the Lord reigns.

Call to Worship (Psalm 149)

Come into God's presence with singing and praise.
> **We join the assembly of faithful followers.**

Bring dancing and melody, joy and laughter.
> **We gather with the great cloud of witnesses**
> **who came before us.**

Sing a new song to God,
even as we remember ancient wisdom.
> **We embrace the saints who died in faith,**
> **as we proclaim the foundation of our hope.**

Opening Prayer (Psalm 149, Luke 6, Ephesians 1)

God of ages past, hope of days yet to come,
> we come into your presence
> > with joy and thanksgiving.

For those who have gone before us,
> we gratefully remember their wisdom.

For those who will follow after us,
> we fervently pray for their growth in faith.

For those who are here now,
>we offer you our lives,
>>that we may be faithful disciples of your love.
In Christ's name, we pray. Amen.

–Or–

Opening Prayer (Luke 6)

God of our forbearers,
>you turn our world upside down.
The world teaches us to trust our wealth,
>our social status, and our reputation,
>>but you teach us that these things
>>>do not lead to life.
The world teaches us to focus on our needs,
>our wants, and our desires,
>>but you teach us to focus on your kingdom,
>>>where the poor, the hungry,
>>>>and the sorrowful receive your blessing.
Help us truly live, as Christ taught us to live,
>that we might follow the example of the saints.
Amen.

Proclamation and Response

Prayer of Yearning (Luke 6:20, 24 NRSV)

Spirit of Truth, open our hearts
>to the fullness of your word.
We long to embrace your compassion:
>"Blessed are you who are poor,
>>for yours is the kingdom of God."
But we shrink from your words of judgment:
>"But woe to you who are rich,
>>for you have received your consolation."

Stir our souls to ease the plight of the poor,
 and curb our desire to soothe our dis-ease
  when we turn away from the needy.
Transform our failings into a fierce resolve
 to bear witness to the fullness of your truth.
Amen.

Words of Assurance (Ephesians 1)

In Christ, we have obtained an inheritance
 of hope and love.
Trust the Lord.
Draw strength from God's grace,
 and be made new in Christ!

Passing the Peace of Christ (All Saints)

Beloved saints, we are all God's children, made one in
Christ Jesus. Let us share signs of unity and love, as we
share the peace of Christ with one another.

Prayer of Preparation (Ephesians 1, Luke 6)

Wisdom on high, may we truly hear your word
 and bear the fruit of its power.
Open the eyes of our hearts,
 that we may discern the hope
  to which we are called.
Set free the spirit striving within us,
 that we may share the riches
  of your powerful love with the world.
Mark us with the seal of your Holy Spirit,
 that we may walk the path of blessedness
  with the saints who came before us. Amen.

Response to the Word (Ephesians 1, Luke 6)

Blessed are you who are poor.

God's kingdom is already in your midst.

Blessed are you who are hungry.

God's abundance is promised to you.

Blessed are you who weep.

God will wipe away your tears.

Blessed are you who are reviled

for living the teaching of our Lord.

You are already saints in God's kingdom.

Blessed are we when we trust God's promises.

May we live in this glorious hope!

–Or–

Response to the Word (Ephesians 1)

We have heard the word of truth,

the gospel of our salvation.

May our hearts be sealed in love

through the power of the Holy Spirit.

And may we be a people who are redeemed

and fitted for the realm of God.

Thanksgiving and Communion

Invitation to the Offering (Luke 6:24 NRSV)

"Woe to you who are rich!" Jesus warns, "for you have received your consolation." To find true consolation and joy in our worldly riches, we must share from our abundance with those who need it most. Come, rich or poor, for you are welcome here. Give, rich or poor, for your gifts are needed by God.

Offering Prayer (Psalm 149, Luke 6)

God of abundant love, hear the song of our hearts—
>a song of thankfulness and praise,
>a song of hope and expectation,
>a song of laughter and joy,
>a song of mirth and good will.

May the song of your love sing forth
>through our tithes and offerings,
>>and through the gift of our very lives.

May the joy of our hearts break forth—
>in acts of comfort to those who weep,
>in acts of mercy to the poor and imprisoned,
>in acts of encouragement to the weary.

We ask this in the name of your Son,
>who opened our hearts to see your love. Amen.

Great Thanksgiving

The Lord be with you.
>**And also with you.**

Lift up your hearts.
>**We lift them up to the Lord.**

Let us give thanks to the Lord our God.
>**It is right to give our thanks and praise.**

It is right, and a good and joyful thing,

>always and everywhere to give thanks to you,
>God of the saints, creator of heaven and earth.

From the ancient dreams of Daniel
>to the journeys of Jesus,
>you have revealed your mighty presence to us.

When your people ignored your dreams and visions,
>and when they placed their trust in earthly kings,
>you came to us as a mighty king,
>revealing the truth and glory of your powerful love.

Through the law and prophets,
     through saints and sinners,
     you have taught us to be your people.
In love and mercy, you speak truth and blessing,
     ever renewing your covenant with us.

And so, with your people on earth,
     and all the company of saints in heaven,
     we praise your name
     and join their unending hymn, saying,
     Holy, holy, holy Lord, God of power and might,
          heaven and earth are full of your glory.
     Hosanna in the highest. Blessed is the one
          who comes in the name of the Lord.
     Hosanna in the highest.

Holy are you and blessed is your holy name.
In the fullness of time, you sent Jesus Christ
     to reveal your powerful love in the world,
     and show us paths of saintliness and holy living.
In humility and love, with justice and power,
     Christ revealed your kingdom,
     and calls us to kingdom living.
Through Christ's powerful love and endless grace,
     we are invited into your presence,
     rescued from our sins, and led on your path
     of justice and righteousness,
     that we may rejoice with the saints of your kingdom.
We, who are both saint and sinner, blessed and cursed,
     come to you in our joys and our sorrows,
     with thanksgiving and hope,
     remembering how Jesus shared bread and wine,
     even when he faced the sinfulness of his disciples.

On the night before his death, Jesus took bread,
    gave thanks to you, broke the bread,
    and gave it to the disciples—
    each of them part saint and part sinner.
Jesus said to every one of them,
    "Take, eat; this is my body that is given for you.
    Do this in remembrance of me."
When the supper was over, Jesus took the cup,
    and giving thanks to you, shared the cup
    with those same imperfect disciples, saying,
    "Drink from this, all of you;
    this is my life in the new covenant,
    poured out for you and for many
    for the forgiveness of sins.
    Do this, as often as you drink it,
    in remembrance of me."

And so, in remembrance of these
    your mighty acts of love and grace,
    we offer ourselves in praise and thanksgiving,
    as saints and sinners in love with you,
    praying for union with Christ,
    even as we proclaim the mystery of faith.
    Christ has died.
    Christ is risen.
    Christ will come again.

Communion Prayer

Pour out your Holy Spirit on us,
and on these gifts of bread and wine.
Make them be for us the life and love of Christ,
that we may be for the world the body of Christ,
redeemed, renewed, and blessed
by your love and grace.
By your Spirit, make us one with Christ,
one with each other,
and one in ministry to all the world.
Bless us until Christ comes in final victory
and we feast at the heavenly banquet
with the saints of your church
and the many touched by your grace.
Through Jesus Christ,
with the Holy Spirit in your holy church,
all honor and glory is yours, almighty God,
now and forevermore. Amen.

Giving the Bread and Cup

(The bread and wine are given to the people, with these
or other words of blessing.)
The life of Christ, living in you.
The love of Christ, flowing through you.

Sending Forth

Benediction (Ephesians 1)

Go in the hope to which Christ calls us.
We will walk the path God sets before us.
Grow in the Spirit's wisdom and truth.
We will live in the love transforming our lives.

–Or–

Benediction (Psalm 149)

Go with God's blessing.
> **God's love surrounds us.**

Go with God's blessing.
> **Christ's joy lifts us.**

Go with God's blessing.
> **The Spirit's hope nurtures us.**

Go with God.

November 6, 2022

Twenty-Second Sunday after Pentecost
Proper 27

B. J. Beu

Color

Green

Scripture Readings

Haggai 1:15b–2:9; Psalm 145:1-5, 17-21;
2 Thessalonians 2:1-5, 13-17; Luke 20:27-38

Theme Ideas

Hope for the future focuses today's readings. Facing distress at the destruction of the temple in Jerusalem, Haggai proclaims that the new temple will be made even greater than the old. The psalmist proclaims that God will save the faithful. The epistle addresses fear over the delay in the Lord's return. As the first fruits of salvation, we have nothing to fear. Finally, Jesus confirms the truth of the resurrection, for our God is the God of the living, not the dead. Those who rise again are like angels who can no longer die. In the midst of anxiety and loss, hope carries the day.

Invitation and Gathering

Centering Words (Psalm 145, 2 Thessalonians 2)

God saves the faithful and hears the cries of the despairing. God comforts our hearts and strengthens our souls in every good work and word.

Call to Worship (Haggai 1, 2 Thessalonians 2)

Though the earth groans and the heavens tremble,
> **God remains faithful.**

Though the seas roar and the winds rage,
> **Christ sees us through.**

Though timbers splinter and walls crumble,
> **The Spirit abides among us.**

–Or–

Call to Worship (Psalm 145)

Praise the Lord our God.
> **Praise God's holy name.**

Proclaim Christ's greatness in the sanctuary.
> **Sing of Christ's mighty deeds among the people.**

Extol the Spirit's protection from the storm.
> **Proclaim the Spirit's grace and mercy.**

Praise the Lord our God.
> **Praise God's holy name.**

Opening Prayer (Haggai 1, Psalm 145, Luke 20)

God of new beginnings, it is a joy to sing your praises.
Your glory blesses our souls with hope.
Your majesty fills our lives with splendor.
Your Spirit makes all things new,
> blessing creation with healing and wholeness.

Shake the heavens and earth once more,
  that we may see your power
    and hold fast to the source of our hope.
For you are greater than our fears,
  and mightier than our failings.
Call us from death to life, Holy One,
  for you are God of the living,
    not the dead. Amen.

Proclamation and Response

Prayer of Yearning (2 Thessalonians 2)
  Reach us in our need, loving God,
    for we wander as lost children
      without your presence in our lives.
  When our hope fails and our confidence is shaken,
    renew us in your mercy.
  When our footsteps falter and our eyesight dims,
    place our feet firmly on the paths of life.
  Remind us that we are your beloved children,
    the handiwork of your gracious love.
  Give us the strength to stand firm
    and hold fast to your promises
      when our courage wanes,
        through Jesus Christ, our Lord. Amen.

Words of Assurance (2 Thessalonians 2)
  Through the Holy Spirit, who is always with us,
    our lives bear the fruit of salvation.
  Through the love of Christ, who is always faithful,
    our sins are forgiven and our lives are made whole.

Passing the Peace (2 Thessalonians 2, Luke 20)

The love of Christ is inexhaustible; the peace of Christ is a gift beyond price. Let us share these gifts with one another today, as we exchange signs of Christ's love and peace.

Response to the Word (2 Thessalonians 2)

God's edicts are as constant as the North Star.
God's precepts are as solid
as the foundations of the earth.
Live the word you have heard this day,
and heed not the advice of scoffers
that would lead you astray.
The Holy Spirit's guidance sanctifies our lives,
that we may bear the fruit of Christ's salvation.

–Or–

Response to the Word (Psalm 145)

Great is the Lord, and greatly to be praised.
Shout God's praises in the sanctuary.
Sing Christ's praises among the people.
Proclaim the Spirit's power to the world.
Great is the Lord, and greatly to be praised.

Thanksgiving and Communion

Offering Prayer (Psalm 145, 2 Thessalonians 2, Luke 20)

Eternal God, you are the caretaker of our souls;
you draw near to all who call on you.
May the offering we bring before you this day
heal the broken lives and unrealized dreams
of our world.

May these gifts be signs of hope for the future,
  especially in places plagued by injustice,
   that all may know the power of your Spirit.
Amen.

Sending Forth

Benediction (Haggai 1)

Go forth with courage, for God is with us.
  God goes with us to guide us.
Go forth with faith, for Christ is with us.
  Christ goes with us to heal us.
Go forth with hope, for the Spirit makes us whole.
  The Spirit goes with us to strengthen us.

November 13, 2022

Twenty-Third Sunday after Pentecost
Proper 28

John Brewer

Color

Green

Scriptures

Isaiah 65:17-25; Isaiah 12; 2 Thessalonians 3:6-13;
Luke 21:5-19

Theme Ideas

The end is near. The end has always been, and will always be, near: the end of the year, the end of a season, the end of heaven and earth as we have known it. Along with the end comes a new beginning—a new heaven and a new earth. God will make this happen. In the meantime, we will be faced with transitions, difficulties, and even persecution for our beliefs. What we consider beautiful, God will tear down. What we consider comfortable, God will disturb. New life comes through change. God has created a universe that is ever changing. Yet, God assures us that a new beginning is near. The new beginning is always near.

Invitation and Gathering

Centering Words

New life comes through change. A new beginning is always near. Embrace the changes God is bringing.

Call to Worship (Isaiah 65)

God will create a new heaven and a new earth.
> **The former things will not be remembered,**
> **nor will they come to mind.**

God rejoices over Jerusalem,
and takes delight in God's people.
> **The sound of weeping and crying**
> **will be heard no more.**

Before we call out, God will answer.
While we are still speaking, God will hear.
> **The wolf and the lamb will feed together,**
> **and the lion will eat straw like the ox.**

They will neither harm nor destroy
on all God's holy mountain.
> **We worship the one who makes all things new.**

–Or–

Call to Worship (Isaiah 12)

Praise the Lord, whose anger has turned away.
> **We will trust and not be afraid.**

The Lord is our strength and our song.
> **God comforts us in our time of need.**

Draw water from the wellspring of eternal life.
> **Surely God is our salvation.**

Sing to the Lord.
> **God has done glorious things.**

Give thanks to the Lord.
> **We will call on God's holy name.**

Opening Prayer (Luke 21)

There is no place to turn, O God,
>for the comfort we desire;
>>no place, but to you alone, O Lord.
Bless us this day,
>that we might be a blessing to others.
Bless us this day,
>that we might be faithful witnesses
>>to life in Christ Jesus,
>>>our redeemer and Lord.
In our songs and prayers,
>in our scriptures and spoken words,
>>reveal your purposes to
>>>through the power of your Holy Spirit.
We are here, O Lord.
Equip us for ministry with the faith and assurance
>only you can provide. Amen.

Proclamation and Response

Prayer of Confession (Luke 21)

We bow before you, O Lord,
>to acknowledge our failings.
We ask forgiveness:
>for words spoken in cruelty,
>for behavior that tears down,
>for failing the ministries of your church,
>for preferring temporal wealth
>>to riches in your Spirit.
Forgive us, we pray,
>and lead us into fullness of life,
>>through Jesus Christ, our Lord. Amen.

Words of Assurance (Isaiah 12)

Surely God is our salvation.
Place your trust in God and do not be afraid,
    for the Lord is our strength and our salvation.
(B. J. Beu)

Passing the Peace

The one who was and is and is to come prepares our
hearts to receive Christ's peace anew. Let us share this
peace with one another.
(B. J. Beu)

Response to the Word (Luke 21)

Lord of the universe, we live in an ever-changing world.
As we embrace the word you have shared with us today,
    show us your steadfast mercy,
        and your unconditional love.
As we seek to live the guidance of your Holy Spirit,
    help us face the competing demands for our loyalty.
As we seek to faithfully follow your Son,
    help us find comfort in your presence,
        for you alone are our help and our salvation.
Amen.

Thanksgiving and Communion

Offering Prayer (Luke 21)

Eternal God, we draw life in your presence.
You have created and sustained us
    to meet the challenges we face each day.
May the gifts and offerings we bring before you
    reflect the light of Christ that shines in our lives,
        a light that can heal the world.

In our living and in our giving,
  help us act in concert with your ways,
   that the world might see in us
    the power of your Spirit. Amen.

Sending Forth

Benediction (2 Thessalonians)

May the strength of God be with you.
May you never tire of the work God calls you to do
  for the benefit of God's kingdom.
Go forth with the power of the Holy Spirit.
Go to share the good news of the gospel
  with everyone you meet,
  for Christ is alive, alive in you! Amen.

November 20, 2022

Twenty-Fourth Sunday after Pentecost
Christ the King / Reign of Christ Sunday
Karin Ellis

Color

White

Scripture Readings

Jeremiah 23:1-6; Luke 1:68-79; Colossians 1:11-20;
Luke 23:33-43

Theme Ideas

On Christ the King Sunday, we celebrate Christ as the
ruler of our lives. Christ does not rule with condemna-
tion, though. Rather, Christ offers forgiveness and rules
like a shepherd, comforting the people and drawing
them closer to God. The "tender mercy of God" spoken
of by Luke is seen throughout the scriptures for this
day. We give thanks for a savior who brings love and
redemption to all.

Invitation and Gathering

Centering Words (Jeremiah 23, Luke 1)

Christ takes care of us, as a shepherd takes care of the
sheep, offering love and redemption, mercy and grace.

Call to Worship (Luke 1)

Our blessed God has gathered us here,
    looking on us with loving eyes.
May we dwell in the tender mercy of God
    as we sing songs of praise.

Opening Prayer (Jeremiah 23, Colossians 1)

Tender Shepherd, you gather us here
    to dwell in your love and grace.
You comfort and guide us.
You heal and redeem us.
As we sing your songs of praise,
    send your light into our lives.
As we commit ourselves to the ways of Christ,
    our guide, ruler, and savior,
        bless us with your presence.
In the name of Christ, we pray. Amen.

Proclamation and Response

Prayer of Confession (Luke 23)

Jesus Christ, Son of God,
    forgive the time we have forgotten you:
        the times we have turned away from you,
        the times we have laughed at you,
        the times we have ignored you
            and the needs of our brothers and sisters.

Bring us close once more,
that we might dwell in your redeeming love.
In your holy name, we pray. Amen.

Words of Assurance (Luke 23:34 NRSV)

Jesus said, "Father, forgive them;
for they do not know what they are doing."
Brothers and sisters, siblings in Christ,
rejoice, for Christ's love and forgiveness is for you!
Amen.

Passing the Peace of Christ (Colossians 1)

The fullness of God dwells in Christ,
the one who brings peace and forgiveness.
The peace of Christ be with you.
And also with you.

Introduction to the Word (Jeremiah 23, Luke 1)

May the great shepherd look favorably upon us,
as we listen to God's story
and share the burdens on our hearts.

Response to the Word (Luke 1, Luke 23)

The Holy Spirit moves us to share God blessings
with the world:
light to those who dwell in darkness,
forgiveness to those who yearn for mercy,
and peace to those who live in conflict.
Let us bring the promise of God's kingdom
to all of God's children.

Thanksgiving

Invitation to the Offering (Jeremiah 23)

The God who shepherds us, comforts us, and provides for us, is the one owed our thanks and gratitude. In deep humility, let us bring our offerings to God.

Offering Prayer (Luke 23)

Almighty Christ, you gave us the gift of yourself.
Now we offer these gifts to you,
 asking that you bless them and use them
 to share you kingdom with all.
In your name, we pray. Amen.

Sending Forth

Benediction (Luke 1, Luke 23)

May God lead us along paths of loving kindness.
May Christ guide our feet in the ways of peace.
May the Spirit send us forth to love and serve others.
Amen.

November 24, 2022

Thanksgiving Day
B. J. Beu

Color

Red

Scripture Readings

Deuteronomy 26:1-11; Psalm 100; Philippians 4:4-9;
John 6:25-35

Theme Ideas

God provides everything we need. In the face of God's
wonderful abundance, we are called to rejoice and celebrate. In our gratitude, Deuteronomy charges us to give
back to God from the first fruits of our harvest. Thanksgiving is a time to focus, not on what we have, but on
what God has given us.

Invitation and Gathering

Centering Words (Psalm 100, Philippians 4)

Rejoice in the Lord always. Again I say, rejoice! For the goodness of God's bounty is sufficient for our needs each day. God's steadfast love never ends.

Call to Worship (Psalm 100)

Make a joyful noise to the Lord, all the earth.
Worship the Lord with gladness.
Come into God's presence with singing.
Enter God's gates with thanksgiving.
Give thanks to the Lord, for God is good.
God's steadfast love endures forever.

–Or–

Call to Worship (Philippians 4)

Rejoice in the Lord always.
Again I say, rejoice!
Thank God for the homes that shelter us.
Rejoice in the Lord always.
Again I say, rejoice!
Thank Christ for the food that nourishes us.
Rejoice in the Lord always.
Again I say, rejoice!
Thank Spirit for the blessings in our lives.
Rejoice in the Lord always.
Again I say, rejoice!

Opening Prayer (Deuteronomy 26, John 25)

Almighty God, you have led us into a land
flowing with milk and honey.

As we rejoice in your manifold blessings,
    turn our thoughts to those who go hungry.
As we celebrate the bounty of your table,
    focus our appetite on food that does not perish.
Help us find our true sustenance in Christ,
    that our souls may never hunger.
And move us to draw our nourishment from him,
    that our spirits may never thirst. Amen.

Proclamation and Response

Prayer of Yearning (Deuteronomy 26)
Almighty God, maker of heaven and earth,
    fill our hearts with gratitude
        on this day of thanksgiving.
You have brought us into a land
    flowing with milk and honey.
You have blessed us with waters
    that well up to eternal life.
Open our mouths to proclaim the bounty
    of your good land,
        for by your power alone do we prosper.
Help us to live each day with true gratitude
    for your many blessings. Amen.

Words of Assurance (Philippians 4)
Let your requests be known to God,
        and Christ will guard our hearts and minds,
        and the Spirit will give us the peace
        that passes all understanding.

Passing the Peace of Christ

As we celebrate God's bounty in our lives, let us give thanks for the blessings of friendship of friends and family. Now let us share this thanksgiving by sharing signs of Christ's peace with one another this day.

Response to the Word (Deuteronomy 26, Philippians 4, John 6)

Rejoice in the Lord always,
and celebrate God's bounty in our lives.
For Christ is our living bread
and his words satisfy our thirsty souls.
Rejoice in the Lord always.
Again I say, rejoice!

Thanksgiving and Communion

Offering Prayer (Deuteronomy 26, John 6)

Bountiful God, we thank and praise you
for your many gifts.
You cause the earth to bring forth food.
You cause rain to kiss the ground to sustain life.
Receive these offerings,
as the first fruit of our labors.
May our gifts be acceptable to you,
and may they go into the world
as signs of our joy and thankfulness.
In Jesus's name, who is the bread of life,
we pray. Amen.

Invitation to Communion (Deuteronomy 26, Philippians 4)

Here, at the Lord's table,
Christ offers us his very self.
We come to the table with thanks and praise.
Here, at this gift of bread and wine,
Christ meets us as honored guests.
We come to the table with songs of joy.
Here, at the foretaste of the heavenly banquet,
Christ calls us his own.
We come to the table of grace.
(From B. J. Beu and Mary Scifres, *Is It Communion Sunday Already?! Communion Resources for All Seasons*)

Sending Forth

Benediction (Philippians 4)

Worry not, but in everything you do,
make your requests known to God.
We go in prayer and supplication,
with thanksgiving and shouts of joy.
May the peace of God, which passes all understanding,
guard your hearts and minds in Christ Jesus, our Lord.
Amen.

November 27, 2022

First Sunday of Advent
Mary Scifres

Color

Purple

Scripture Readings

Isaiah 2:1-5; Psalm 122; Romans 13:11-14;
Matthew 24:36-44

Theme Ideas

Time to wake up! The advent of God is near, and to-day's scriptures call us to draw closer to God, as we prepare for God's arrival in our midst. Whether we are gathering on a high mountain, preparing our homes for an unexpected visitor, or dressing ourselves in Christ's very presence, these scriptures invite us to prepare with attentiveness and intentionality. Time to wake up. The advent of God is near!

Invitation and Gathering

Centering Words (Romans 13, Matthew 24)
Wake up! God is near. Wake up! God is here.

Call to Worship (Isaiah 2, Psalm 122, Romans 13)
Come, let's go together to God's mountain—
a mountain of God's glory and peace.
Let's prepare for Christ's arrival—
the birth of the prince of peace.
Come, let's worship the Spirit of love.
Clothed in Christ's love,
we are ready to worship and pray.

Opening Prayer (Psalm 122, Romans 13, Matthew 24)
Draw near to us, O God,
even as we draw near to you.
Open our hearts and our minds to your presence,
and wake us up from the sleep and inattention
holding us back.
Prepare us to receive your love,
even as we prepare our lives
to celebrate the joy of Christ's birth.
In joyful hope, we pray. Amen.

Proclamation and Response

Prayer of Yearning (Isaiah 2, Romans 13, Matthew 24)
Even when we're tired, Lord,
we long to awake to your presence.

Even when we're distracted,
    we yearn to be held spellbound by your power.
Even when we're lost and wander away from you,
    we hope to rest safely in the arms of your grace.
Wake us from sleep, O God;
    reveal your love and mercy,
        and grant us the peace of your redemption.
In humble gratitude, we pray. Amen.

Words of Assurance (Psalm 122, Romans 13)

In God's love, we find rest.
In Christ's grace, we receive forgiveness.
In the Spirit's presence, we know peace.
Thanks be to God.

Passing the Peace of Christ (Psalm 122)

Even as we pray for the peace of the world, let us bring peace to one another, as we share the peace of Christ this day.

Introduction to the Word (Isaiah 2)

Come, let's go to the mountain of God.
Let's climb to the heights of God's holy word,
    that God may teach us holy ways
    and guide us on righteous paths.

Response to the Word (Psalm 122, Romans 13, Matthew 24)

Prince of peace, we pray for peace this day,
    not just for Jerusalem,
        but for the entire world.
We pray for your peace in our own lives,
    that we may know the peace
        that passes all understanding.

We pray for your peace in our minds,
>	that we may be quiet enough to hear your voice
>		and know your ways.
We pray for your peace in our schedules,
>	that we may prepare and receive your arrival,
>		not just at Christmas,
>			but every day of every year. Amen.

Thanksgiving and Communion

Offering Prayer (Isaiah 2, Psalm 122)

Gracious God, as we bring our gifts to you,
>	we bring much more than earthly treasure;
>	we bring our very lives.
Transform us through our giving,
>	that we may grow ever closer to you.
Help us share your peace and love with others
>	as joyfully and generously,
>		as you have shared your gifts with us.
In your holy name, we pray. Amen.

Invitation to Communion (Isaiah 2)

Come, let's go up to God's holy mountain,
>	the mountain of love revealed to us in Christ Jesus.
Let's go to join the feast of grace
>	shown to us at this table of holy communion.
Come to this abundant feast, this mountain of love,
>	that our hearts and minds may be prepared
>	to receive the coming Christ.

Sending Forth

Benediction (Psalm 122)

Peace be with you,
and also with you.
Go forth to bring peace to the world.

December 4, 2022

Second Sunday of Advent
B. J. Beu

Color

Purple

Scripture Readings

Isaiah 11:1-10; Psalm 72:1-7, 18-19; Romans 15:4-13;
Matthew 3:1-12

Theme Ideas

Isaiah promises that a righteous branch will grow out of
the shoot of Jesse—a branch that will bring justice and
peace to all of creation. In Lent, Christians prepare to
receive this branch in the birth of Jesus. Matthew warns
that the peace promised by Isaiah will be accompanied
by the destruction of the wicked. Indeed, the axe is already lying at the root of the tree. In the name of the one
who baptizes us with fire and the Holy Spirit, it is time
to lead lives worthy of repentance. Such living promises
us hope for the future.

Invitation and Gathering

Centering Words (Isaiah 11)

A righteous branch grows out of the root of Jesse—a branch that brings justice and peace. Let us prepare our hearts to receive the blessings of this branch in our lives and in our world.

Call to Worship (Isaiah 11)

A shoot has come forth from the stump of Jesse.
The spirit of the Lord rests upon his shoulders.
Wisdom guides his feet.
Righteousness is the belt around his waist.
Faithfulness is the mantle upon his shoulders.
Counsel and might cover his head.
A shoot has come forth from the stump of Jesse.
God's promised salvation is at hand.

–Or–

Call to Worship (Matthew 3)

Prepare the way of the Lord.
God's kingdom has drawn near.
Prepare the way of peace.
God's salvation is at hand.
Prepare the way of righteousness.
God's Spirit moves among us.
Prepare the way of the Lord.
**Blessed is the one who comes
in the name of the Lord.**

Opening Prayer (Isaiah 11, Psalm 72)

Mighty One, the spirit of the Lord
    rests upon your chosen one:
        the spirit of wisdom and understanding,
        the spirit of counsel and might,
        the spirit of knowledge
          and the fear of the Lord.
As we behold your glory in the heavens,
    breathe your passion for justice into our hearts,
        that we may defend the poor,
          deliver the oppressed,
            and help the weary.
In this season of Advent,
    may your righteousness flourish
        and may your peace abound,
          that none shall hurt or destroy
            on all your holy mountain. Amen.

Proclamation and Response

Prayer of Yearing (Matthew 3)

Living God, we long to wake from sleep,
    for your kingdom has drawn near.
Already, the axe is lying at the foot of the tree,
    and we yearn to return to you once more.
May our spirits bear the fruit of repentance.
We desire the blessings to be found
    when we respond to the prophets of old
        by dedicating our lives to you
          in word and deed. Amen.

Words of Assurance (Psalm 72, Romans 15)

Hold fast to the promises of God—
   promises of steadfast love and forgiveness.
Abide in the grace of Christ.
Rest in the power of the Holy Spirit.
Do this and you will know life eternal.

Passing the Peace of Christ (Romans 15)

Welcome one another, as Christ has welcomed you.
Greet one another with signs of peace, as Christ has welcomed you with the peace that passes all understanding.

Response to the Word (Isaiah 11, Romans 15, Matthew 3)

A righteous branch was promised
and a righteous branch was given.
   What was written in former days
   has become our source of hope and consolation.
We have heard judgment proclaimed,
and we have witnessed salvation draw near.
   Thanks be to God.
   Praise be to Christ.
   And glory be to the Holy Spirit.

Thanksgiving and Communion

Invitation to Offering (Psalm 72)

Marvelous are the gifts of God's grace. Let us respond with wonder and delight by offering our very selves back to God. With reverence and devotion, let us give generously of our gifts, that through our offerings, God's promises might be fulfilled.

Offering Prayer (Isaiah 11)

Gracious God, you offer us a gift beyond price.
Your Son is like the sweet kiss of rain
    on a barren land.
Your promised salvation is like the bread of heaven
    for those who are perishing.
In gratitude for your abundant gifts,
    we commit ourselves to act justly,
        in solidarity with the poor,
    and we pledge our assistance
        to those who are in need.
May the gifts we bring before you this day
    hasten the day when none shall hurt or destroy
        on all your holy mountain. Amen.

Sending Forth

Benediction (Psalm 72, Romans 15)

Live in harmony with one another,
    through the hope we find in Christ Jesus.
Act with righteousness and peace,
    that justice may flourish, and peace may abound.
Love with hope and grace,
    that joy may fill your days
    like sunshine on a cold winter's day.

December 11, 2022

Third Sunday of Advent
Mary Scifres

Color

Purple

Scripture Readings

Isaiah 35:1-10; Luke 1:47-55; James 5:7-10;
Matthew 11:2-11

Theme Ideas

Joy emerges, even in the driest desert. Joy emerges,
even after the greatest suffering. Joy emerges in each of
today's scriptures, whether the blind find sight or the
hungry are filled with good things. Joy is the hope to
which we are called in today's readings. Joy is the promise that Christmas personifies when a tiny child, born
to a humble working-class couple, arrives to proclaim
God's presence in our midst. Joy to the world on this
third Sunday of Advent.

Invitation and Gathering

Centering Words (Isaiah 35, Luke 1)

Even in our weakness, Christ arrives with strength and courage. Even in our sorrow, Christmas comes to bring hope and joy. May this promise take root in our souls, as we wait with patience for Christ and Christmas to arrive.

Call to Worship (Isaiah 35, Luke 1, James 5)

Rejoice! God's promises are ever near.
We wait for Christ's birth with patience.
Rejoice! God's strength is with us.
We rest in the power of God's mighty love.
Rejoice! We gather in the joy of our salvation.
In this love, we gather to worship and pray.

Opening Prayer (Isaiah 35, James 5)

Promised One, enter our hearts anew.
Enter our worship with your promised presence,
    that we may know you better.
Enter our lives and our world,
      that we may proclaim your presence
        and sing your praises.
With joyous gratitude, we pray in your blessed name.
Amen.

Proclamation and Response

Prayer of Yearning (Isaiah 35, James 5)

God of promise, be with us in our hour of need.
Grant us hope,
    when despair overwhelms us.

Grant us healing and mercy,
 when illness and injury sap our strength.
Grant us life and growth,
 when death and stagnation threaten us.
Grant us patience and perseverance,
 when we grow weary of awaiting
  the coming of your kingdom.
In Christ's holy name, we pray. Amen.

Words of Assurance (Isaiah 35)

In Christ's mercy and grace,
 God's ransomed ones return.
In Christ's love and faithfulness,
 everlasting happiness and joy flow abundantly
 and forgiveness and mercy make us whole.

Response to the Word or Call to Worship (Isaiah 35, Luke 1)

Be strong, even in your weakness.
 Christ will be our strength.
Find hope, even in your despair.
 Christ arrives to bring us hope.
Embrace joy, even in the face of sorrow.
 Christ, our joy, is coming soon.

Thanksgiving and Communion

Invitation to the Offering (Luke 1)

Rejoice, for God has done great things for us. In gratitude, let us bring our gifts to God this day.

Offering Prayer (Luke 1)

God of promises and joy, receive these gifts
>we return to you now.
Bless this offering,
>that our gifts may be signs of joy and hope
>>for others in need.

Sending Forth

Benediction (Isaiah 35, Luke 1)

As children of God's promise,
>we go now to bring hope to the world.
Blessed by Christ's presence,
>we go forth in joy and love.

December 18, 2022

Fourth Sunday of Advent
Kirsten Linford

Color

Purple

Scripture Readings

Isaiah 7:10-16; Psalm 80:1-7, 17-19; Romans 1:1-7; Matthew 1:18-25

Theme Ideas

In their own ways, both Isaiah and the psalmist point toward the coming of Christ. Isaiah's words were often understood as a prophecy, and that is likely how the sources of Matthew saw it. But prophecies only have meaning if we choose to follow them. Perhaps the most powerful part of the Mathew passage is in Joseph's response to the angel's visit. He chooses to welcome Jesus into his family, making a promise to the one who will come as God's promise. The Christ child will be adopted, as well as begotten. Psalm 80 names both the hope and the promise of a new life that saves us and restores us. On this fourth Sunday of Advent, it is worth remembering that new life comes to us, but we have to be willing to choose it. We have to receive it and make our own promise to live it.

Invitation and Gathering

Centering Words (Isaiah 7, Matthew 1)
Look, the young woman is with child and shall bear a son. You shall name him Immanuel. When Joseph awoke from sleep, he did as the angel of the Lord commanded. Today, the promise of new life comes to us. How will *we* receive it? How will *we* claim it? How will *we* live it?

Call to Worship (Psalm 80)
O God, hear our call.
> **Stir up your strength and come to save us!**
Restore us, O God.
> **Let your face shine, that we may be saved.**
For we know that new life is coming.
> **A child will change us all.**
Let your hand be upon him in blessing.
> **For he will bring you near.**
He will be God-with-us.
> **Give us life, O God,**
> **and we will forever call on your name.**

Opening Prayer
Holy One, you send us new life in so many forms.
Open our minds,
> that we may recognize it.
Open our hearts,
> that we may receive it.
Open our bodies,
> that we may embrace it.

Open our souls,
  that we may live it.
Open us this day and all days. Amen.

Proclamation and Response

Prayer of Confession (Isaiah 7, Romans 1, Matthew 1)

O God, you bring us life in ways we do not even realize,
  in forms we do not always understand.
We are so busy,
  the moments moving faster each day.
We do not always pay attention to your presence
  when it comes.
Often we cannot see what is right in front of us.
  We are asleep, even when awake.
And grace slips by us, unrecognized and unrequited.
We miss the opportunity to find you in one another.
We waste our chances for love.
We put you to the test, not with our unbelief,
  but with our distraction.
We think we are too busy for you.
But you, God, still choose us.
You take our struggles and turn them into strengths,
  calling us apostles, making us friends.
You put your own self right into our hands,
  trusting that we can notice your gifts,
    recognize their meaning,
      and make a place for them in our lives.
Forgive us, God, for our distractions.
Slow our stride and calm our souls.

Remind our busy brains
that there is nothing we have to do
to be loved by you,
nothing we have to make or even be.
For your new life is coming even now,
awaiting to make us whole. Amen.

Words of Assurance (Romans 1)

To the weak and the strong, Christ comes.
To the old and the young, Christ appears.
To the lost and the found, Christ arrives.
Christ makes us apostles and offers us grace.
Christ makes us friends with each other and with him.
He makes us family and welcomes us home.

Passing the Peace of Christ (Romans 1)

Grace to you, and peace from God, our creator, and from
Jesus, the Christ. Let us share such greetings of grace
and peace with one another.

Prayer of Preparation (Psalm 19)

May the words of my mouth
and the meditations of our hearts
be acceptable in your sight, O Lord,
our strength and our redeemer. Amen.

Response to the Word (Matthew 1)

God of grace, you put on flesh
and come to live among us.
You make us new in a million ways each day.
You never hesitate to become small and vulnerable,
fitting into each heart, each life.
May your word fit into our hearts this day,
and may it grow until it is born anew in our lives,
ready to make us whole once more.

Thanksgiving and Communion

Offering Prayer (Psalm 80)

Gracious One, you have restored us
    in body and in soul.
You have given us abundant life,
    more than we could have ever imagined.
You have made your face shine upon us
    to make us whole.
Holy One, bless now the offerings
    of our hearts and lives,
        that we might shine as you shine,
            and share your blessings with others.
Amen.

Sending Forth

Benediction (Romans 1)

Beloved, welcome the grace of God,
    as you welcome the coming of Christ.
Go in peace to love and serve.

December 24, 2022

Christmas Eve

B. J. Beu

Color

White

Scripture Readings

Isaiah 9:2-7; Psalm 96; Titus 2:11-14; Luke 2:1-20

Theme Ideas

Today's theme is joy, for salvation has arrived. Isaiah rejoices that the people who walked in darkness have seen a great light. God's glory has been made manifest in the birth of child called Wonderful Counselor, Mighty God, Everlasting Father, Prince of Peace. God's justice shall be established forever, and the world will be a place of righteousness. The epistle and Gospel readings identify this child as God's Son, Jesus Christ. Hear the good news. Christ is born. In Christ, we find the fulfillment of our Advent expectations: peace, hope, love, and joy.

Invitation and Gathering

Centering Words (Isaiah 9)

Walk no longer in darkness, for the light of the world
has come.

Call to Worship (Psalm 96)

Sing to the Lord a new song.
> **Dance before the Lord, all the earth.**

Declare God's glory among the nations.
> **Proclaim God's salvation to the peoples.**

For great is the Lord,
> **and greatly to be praised.**

Come! Let us worship.

–Or–

Call to Worship (Luke 2)

Sing, choirs of angels.
> **Sing in exaltation.**

Let the shepherds in the fields rejoice.
> **Let the stars in the sky**
> **worship the newborn king.**

For heaven has come down to earth.
> **Salvation has come to our homes this day.**

Sing, choirs of angels.
> **Sing in exaltation.**

Opening Prayer (Luke 2)

God of love, choirs of angels sang to your glory
> on the night of Jesus's birth.

Open our mouths to sing your praise,
> that we might join the heavenly chorus.

As the shepherds left their sheep in the fields
    may we leave our cares behind,
        that we too may find the hope of our salvation
            in the Christ child.
On this most holy of nights,
    may our worship befit the Prince of Peace,
        who came to show us the depths of your love.
Amen.

Proclamation and Response

Prayer of Yearing (Isaiah 9, Luke 2)

Source of joy, you are the author of everlasting life.
Touch us with the wonder of that holy night
    when your Son came into the world.
For we yearn to leave the shadows behind
    to walk in darkness no more.
We long to behold your light shining in our lives,
    as it shined in the stars above
        on the night love came down at Christmas.
Guide our steps to the manger,
    and make us instruments of your justice and peace,
        that the gift of your salvation
            may reside in every corner of the globe.
We ask this in the name of our Wonderful Counselor,
    Mighty God, Everlasting Father, Prince of Peace.
Amen.

Words of Assurance (Isaiah 9)

Like the people of old, we, who walked in darkness,
  have seen a great light.
We, who dwelt in a land of deep darkness,
  on us light has shined.
Live in this light and you will live indeed.

Passing the Peace of Christ (Isaiah 9, Luke 2)

Glory to God in the highest! Let earth receive her king.
Let us share signs of peace, as we celebrate the birth of
the Prince of Peace on this holy night.

Response to the Word (Isaiah 9)

Once we walked in darkness.
  But now we dwell in everlasting light.
For the Christ child is with us.
  Our salvation is at hand.
He is called Wonderful Counselor, Mighty God,
  Everlasting Father, Prince of Peace.
Leave the darkness behind.
  Our light has come.

Thanksgiving and Communion

Invitation to Offering (Luke 2)

What can we offer to God in return for the gift of Christ
Jesus? We can offer our love, our joy, our hope, our
peace. We can offer our commitment to share these gifts
with the ones Jesus came to serve and to save.

Offering Prayer (Luke 2)

God of surprise and wonder,
  you came in a way no one expected.
When we looked for you in power and might,
  you came in weakness and vulnerability.
As we worship you anew this night/day,
  open our hearts to those you came to save—
    especially the least and the lost.
May the gifts we offer into your service
  continue the work you began in a manger
    so many years ago. Amen.

Sending Forth

Benediction (Isaiah 9, Luke 2)

Walk in darkness no longer.
  We will walk in the light of Christ.
Sing of Christ's birth with the choirs of angels.
  We will sing with the heavenly host.
Go and proclaim the good news.
  Jesus Christ is born.

–Or–

Benediction (Luke 2, Titus 2)

Go to the manger of love.
For God's love has brought us salvation.
Christ's grace has given us hope.
The Spirit's mercy has made us servants
  of the Prince of Peace.
Go with God.

December 25, 2022

Christmas Day

Joanne Reynolds

Color

White

Scripture Readings

Isaiah 52:7-10; Psalm 98; Hebrews 1:1-4, 5-12; John 1:1-14

Theme Ideas

Rescue, return, rejoicing, and recognition are the themes running through these scriptures. Reflecting forward, the prophet Isaiah and the psalmist foresaw the incarnation as an act that would expand God's salvation from the family of the chosen people to the wider world, one that the entire creation would greet with rejoicing (Isaiah 52 and Psalm 98). The letter to the Hebrews and the opening verses of John's Gospel reflect backward to this historic moment, placing Jesus as both the eternal and the human embodiment of the divine presence, the one who we must rightfully worship.

Invitation and Gathering

Centering Words (Luke 2:28-32 NRSV)

Simeon took him in his arms and praised God, saying, "Master, now you are dismissing your servant in peace, according to your word; for my eyes have seen your salvation . . . a light for revelation to the Gentiles and for glory to your people Israel."

Call to Worship (John 1, Psalm 98)

In the beginning was the Word,
and the Word was with God,
and the Word was God.
>**Make a joyful noise to the Lord, all the earth.**
>**Let the seas roar and the mountains quake.**
Everything came into being through the Word.
What came into being was life,
and the life was the light for all people.
>**Sing to the Lord a new song,**
>**for God has done marvelous things.**
The Word became flesh and blood,
and lived among us to bring all people to the light.
>**Let heaven and earth break forth into joyous song,**
>**singing praises to our God.**
The light shines in the darkness
and the darkness has not overcome it.
>**Christ, our light, shines forth in glory.**
>**Christ, our life, brings grace and truth.**
Let us worship. Alleluia!
(B. J. Beu)

Opening Prayer

Incarnate One, we bow before you on this day
 to celebrate the coming of your presence among us.
You are the fulfillment of God's ancient promises,
 a living testimony to God's faithfulness.
We thank you for your life-transforming love:
 you are a gift of sustenance
  to souls who hunger and thirst;
 you are balm to the wounded
  and strength to the lame;
 you are the very light of God,
  shining for all the nations to see.
With all creation, we rejoice at your coming,
 as we worship before your manger/cradle.

Proclamation and Response

Prayer of Confession

All-seeing and all-merciful God,
 Christmas day always seems to catch us off guard.
Instead of moving in concert
 with the peace of your coming,
  we have exhausted ourselves
   dancing to the world's tune.
Instead of making time and space for your presence,
 we have spent our energy on physical,
  rather than heavenly endeavors.
Instead of grasping the awe of your coming,
 we have allowed sheer busy-ness
  to batter all wonder from our lives.
Forgive us, we pray.

In your mercy, help us to reclaim
>   the marvel and mystery of your birth.
In your grace, help us encounter you once again
>   in the great rhythms of creation, incarnation,
>   >   and salvation. Amen
(B. J. Beu)

Words of Assurance (Psalm 98, Hebrews 1)

With righteousness and equity,
>   Christ has come to bring justice and grace,
>   love and compassion.
Through the tender mercies of our God,
>   and the glorious love of Christ Jesus,
>   we are forgiven.
(B. J. Beu)

Passing the Peace of Christ (Isaiah 52)

How beautiful are the feet of those who come announcing peace. How radiant are the eyes of those who shine with the light of God's love. With blessings of peace and love to share, let us turn to one another and offer signs of God's blessings this Christmas day.
(B. J. Beu)

Response to the Word

The incarnation and the manger leave us with this inescapable truth: in grace, God was pleased to come among us. God sent Jesus into the world, that the world might be saved through him. Let us live according to this good news.

Thanksgiving and Communion

Invitation to the Offering (Matthew 2)

When the wise men saw the child with Mary his mother, they knelt down and paid him homage, offering gifts of gold, frankincense, and myrrh. Let us follow their example, as we bring our offerings to the Christ child.

Offering Prayer

O God, in this sacred season,
> we offer you these treasures from our stores,
>> along with the gift of our hearts.

We place these gifts on your altar
> to help build the kingdom you opened to us
>> on this day of Christ's birth.

We lift our hearts to you,
> even as we place our lives into your care,
>> as we follow your Son,
>>> who is the way, the truth, and the life.

Amen.

Sending Forth

Benediction

Go out now with joy and peace,
hearing the mountains and hills break forth in song.
We will sing with the trees of the forest
and shout for joy with the flowers in the fields.
Go forth with thanksgiving to the Father, the Son,
and Holy Spirit, one God, Mother and Father of us all.

Benediction (Isaiah 52, Psalm 98, John 1)

Make a joyful noise to the Lord.
We will sing praises to our God.
Walk in the light of Christ.
We will share the joy of God's holy love.
Be messengers of hope and peace.
We will proclaim the good news.
Christ is born. Alleluia!

(B. J. Beu)

Contributors

B. J. Beu is a pastor, spiritual director, and coach who has served churches in the United Church of Christ for over twenty-five years. B. J. lives in Laguna Beach with his wife, Mary, and enjoy spending time with their son, Michael, who works nearby as a filmmaker for churches and small businesses.

Mary Petrina Boyd is pastor of Marysville United Methodist Church, northeast of Seattle. She spends alternating summers working as an archaeologist in Jordan.

Joanne Carlson Brown is a United Methodist minister serving Des Moines UMC in the state of Washington. She lives with Brigid, her beloved Westie.

John Brewer has recently retired after serving forty-five years as a United Methodist pastor in the Pacific Northwest, including six years as a District Superintendent. Married for fifty-six years to Sharon Streich Brewer, they enjoy time with their three children, seven grandchildren and two great-grandchildren.

Robin D. Dillon is a pastor in the East Ohio Conference of the United Methodist Church.

James Dollins is Senior Pastor of Anaheim United Methodist Church in Southern California, where he lives with his wife, Serena, and sons, Forrest and Silas. He is a lover of music, intercultural ministries, and God's creation.

Karin Ellis is a United Methodist pastor who lives with her husband and children in La Cañada, California. She enjoys writing liturgy for worship and children's stories.

Rebecca J. Kruger Gaudino, a United Church of Christ minister in Portland, Oregon, teaches biblical studies and theology at the University of Portland and also writes for the Church.

Jaime D. Greening, in addition to being the pastor of Fellowship Baptist Church in Marble Falls, Texas writes blogs, worship materials, and wonderful fiction stories about Pastor Butch Gregory. Visit his site at https://jamiegreening.com.

Bill Hoppe, a friend of Aslan, has recently retired to North Carolina after many years as the music director and keyboardist at Bear Creek UMC in Woodinville, Washington.

Kirsten Linford grew up in Red Rock Christian Church in Boise, Idaho and has strong Disciples roots. She is currently the pastor of Westwood Hills Congregational Church (UCC) in Los Angeles. Active in both the Disciples and UCC churches, she has served on committees at both the association/conference and national levels. Kirsten shares her life with her young daughter, Riley, and their golden retriever, Seamus.

Catarina Paton studied music and worship at Azusa Pacific University. She works in worship production at churches in southern California, but remains a member of Laguna Beach United Methodist Church.

Joanne Reynolds is a hymn poet who worships with Congregational churches that are members of the United Church of Christ—Corona del Mar, California, Crested Butte, Colorado, and Scituate, Massachusetts.

Mary J. Scifres is a United Methodist pastor, coach, consultant, author and motivational speaker who brings both inspiration and expertise for twenty-first-century leadership in creative worship, church growth, change management, visioning, and strategic planning. Learn more at www.maryscifres.com.

Deborah Sokolove is Professor of Art and Worship at Wesley Theological Seminary, where she also serves as the Director of the Henry Luce III Center for the Arts and Religion.

Mark Sorensen is Lead Pastor for The Harvest Contemporary Service at Woodlands United Methodist Church in Texas. Married to his best friend, Mark and Nycole recently celebrated their twenty-seventh wedding anniversary.

Michelle L. Torigian is a pastor in the United Church of Christ and blogs at michelletorigian.com.

Scripture Index